The
Independent
Walker's Guide
to
France

Other titles in the series

*The Independent Walker's Guide to
Great Britain*

The Independent Walker's Guide to Italy

The
Independent
Walker's Guide
to
France

by Frank Booth

*35 Extraordinary Walks
in 16 of France's Finest Regions*

114580

INTERLINK BOOKS
NEW YORK

First published in 1996 by

INTERLINK BOOKS
An imprint of Interlink Publishing Group, Inc.
99 Seventh Avenue
Brooklyn, New York 11215

Library of Congress Cataloging-in-Publication Data

Booth, Frank W., 1951–
　The independent walker's guide to France / by Frank Booth.
　　p. cm. — (The independent walker series)
　"35 Extraordinary walks in 16 of France's finest regions."
　Includes index.
　ISBN 1–56656–184–1 (pb)
　1. France—Guidebooks.　2. Walking—France—Tours.
3. Automobile travel—France—Guidebooks.　4. Landscape—
France—Guidebooks.　5. France—Maps, Tourist.　I. Title.
II. Series.
DC 16.B7 1996
914.404'839—dc20　　　　　　　　　　　　　　　　95–38193
　　　　　　　　　　　　　　　　　　　　　　　　　　CIP

Printed and bound in the United States of America
10 9 8 7 6 5 4 3 2 1

Contents

Part One: Hitting the Trail

1. Before You Leave

2. When You Get There

3. Trail Life

Part Two: 35 Great Walks

Contents

Preface

Le Puy-en-Velay. We emerged from the train looking like Rocky Mountaineers—capacious backpacks loaded and bristling with every piece of high-tech camping equipment that we could afford. I was carrying at least sixty pounds, including camp stove and freeze-dried food, my wife somewhat less but still wobbling under the weight of an unfamiliar pack. We would not have been an unusual sight in the Alps, but here in the heart of central France we were definitely out of place—there were no other mountain packs in sight.

Our goal was to walk along the Chemin St. Jacques (the pilgrimage trail to Santiago de Compostela) until we reached Conques, about 125 miles down the road. We had travelled in France several times before and had done a variety of backpacking trips in North America. Was it possible to combine walking and France together? That was the question.

A couple of years earlier, I had acquired, by chance, two books written for English hikers who dared to venture into France, and the idea was born. My desire to walk in France grew slowly from mild curiosity to total obsession. Both of my books contained numerous color photos of a remarkably beautiful land traversed by many mysterious trails that led to great adventures. I would sit at night studying the photos and imagining myself walking through these ethereal landscapes dotted by quaint villages and unique historical sites. Finally, I could no longer restrain myself, and that is how we ended up in Le Puy-en-Velay.

The practical information contained in my wonderful picture books was barely adequate for an American to plunge into the intricacies of the French walking world. However, in a two-day Paris adventure, I did manage to acquire a guide to the trail and some appropriate maps. Even with the guide and maps, I still had some doubts about the practicality of this undertaking. Could we really walk from one town to the next without getting lost? Could we find a place to stay, something to eat? Were there great dangers in getting way off the beaten tourist path? All of these questions, and many more, permeated my thoughts. The events of our first day confirmed some of my doubts; we did end up lost and away from our planned route. However, we did find a place to stay, something to eat, and a ride the next morning by the gracious innkeeper back to the vicinity of the trail. It also turned out that my paranoia about being able to find food and lodging, which led to the sixty-pound backpack, was unfounded. I did not need to carry much at all—although it is possible to backpack and camp if you wish. Several years and many hundreds of miles later, I have learned much about walking in France. The following pages are filled with useful information that I wish had been available to me during that first day and on many subsequent days of sometimes difficult but always rewarding walking.

Introduction

Although this is a walkers' guide, it is also about escaping and avoiding the DROPS. The DROPS are not a communicable disease. They are something far more insidious: the DREADED OTHER PEOPLE who are always in your way, going where you want to go when you want to go. You have seen them everywhere—in long lines at the bank, at the supermarket with bounteous baskets standing six deep in front of you, and in disabled vehicles blocking your path during interminable rush-hour traffic. Great multitudes of DROPS are waiting for you in France.

Seldom will you see a single DROP (perhaps this word can only be used in the plural; a single individual may not qualify for DROPhood). They tend to cluster in large numbers around people who are trying to avoid them. Like stampeding cattle, they destroy everything in their path. International publications are currently reporting the results of their rampaging: as *Newsweek* put it in July 1992, "These days it is tough to find a vacation spot that doesn't in some way resemble a shopping mall, a garbage dump, or a traffic jam."

Even with this book in hand, you will not always be able to avoid the DROPS, but you will have a strategy to retain your independence and sanity. For example, if you are in Paris, you will want to visit Louis XIV's monumental *château* at Versailles. In the palace, you will be shoulder to shoulder with DROPS; however, when you leave Versailles do not allow yourself to be herded into a bus or train for a quick commute back to Paris. Take the six-mile walk through forests and around lakes to the sleepy town of St-Cyr-l'Ecole, where you can take a fast train back to Paris (see Walk 32). You will probably spend less time along the trail than you did in line at Versailles, and you will see none of the

DROPS whose elbows you encountered at Versailles.

On the Mediterranean Sea, near Saint-Tropez, you can lie cheek to cheek with the beautiful bodies that grace the crowded but famous plage de Pampelonne. When, and if, you become weary of body inspecting, you can take a seven-mile walk along a ruggedly beautiful trail that skirts the coast all the way into Saint-Tropez (Walk 19). The trail alternates between rocky, steep terrain and sandy beaches. Between beaches, you will see few other people. Although some of the beaches along the way are crowded, others, remote from vehicular access, are sometimes abandoned. You can pass an entire day walking and swimming your way back to Saint-Tropez.

This book shows you how to walk between and around sites that are endlessly written about in ordinary guides. The trails described in this book will take you to many of France's most famous monuments and also to a variety of lesser known but equally interesting areas. You will see the French going about their daily lives on farms, in villages, and along roads too remote to appear on most maps. Local cows, horses, sheep, chickens, and dogs will often be present to greet you.

This book is organized into two sections. The first part, Hitting the Trail, provides general information on travel to France and what to expect when you arrive: from how to use public transportation and driving tips to information about hotels and restaurants. And of course it also supplies you with all the information you need to become a successful *randonneur* (the French word for walker or hiker). The second section contains practical information about thirty-five great walks, including distance, time duration, and a general description of the trail and local sights. Each walk description also has an accompanying set of trail notes and maps that will alert you to possible problems and confusion along the route, and help you plot your course through undiscovered France.

Walking as Opposed to Other Forms of Travel

Why not rent a car or take a train or a bus or even pedal a bicycle? Why walk? There are faster ways of getting around, and if you go faster, you can see more. I understand this mentality and have been on some breathtaking driving tours of Europe, hurtling down expressways from sight to sight at one hundred miles per hour while German cars pass at warp speed. If this will be the extent of your vacation, driving quickly between famous sites, stay home, rent a travel video about France, and save money.

Although I recommend travel by car, you should also take the time for frequent walks. When you walk, you create unique memories, avoid the DROPS, and seldom see any mechanized form of transportation. All of these are luxuries afforded to few twentieth-century travellers.

Trains and buses in France are generally very good, and you will want to use these modes of transportation as an aid to your walking. However, I would not recommend spending valuable vacation time riding around on crowded public transportation, particularly during the summer months when the DROPS assemble en masse. When you take a train or a bus, you often miss the most important part of your trip—the trail or what lies between your destinations. There are no surprises on public transportation, and you will probably have numerous DROPS and dirty windows separating you from what you came to see: France.

Some people extol the virtues of bicycling in Europe. Yes, you will get some exercise, and you will see some interesting monuments. You will not, however, get far off the beaten path; bicycles go where cars go—where everyone else goes. The roads that cyclists pedal are less frequented by motorized vehicles but by no means untravelled. Many of these roads are very narrow, almost too narrow for two cars and too narrow for two cars and a bicycle. The traffic in Europe almost always goes at breakneck pace and there is very little reverence for cyclists. Furthermore, European cars are notorious for their choking emissions and high-decibel noise. On a trail, you will encounter none of these difficulties.

The Independent Walker

This book is designed to help you, an independent traveller, plan a walking tour of France. There is no single way of walking in France, and whether you are relying on your thumb for locomotion and sleeping in an army-surplus pup tent or leasing a Mercedes to shuttle yourself between multi-starred luxury hotels, you will find this book to be worth more than you paid for it.

All of the walks have been selected according to the following criteria: the walk itself is of great visual delight; the trail is near a noteworthy tourist sight or in an area of great natural beauty; there is easy access to public transportation. As an added bonus, all of the walks are along France's renowned and well-organized system of public trails, where you will always be safe and be able to find your way without becoming lost. Finally, another unique feature of this book is that all of the walks are linear; you will not find yourself walking around in circles (i.e., getting nowhere). Linear walks are interesting throughout their entire length, whereas circular walks, which you will find in other walking guides, usually include a less-than-attractive or repetitious return to the starting point. Linear walks also impart a feeling of accomplishment in having arrived at a town or city in the traditional way of our ancestors, on foot. At Cahors, for example, you will begin the day as a medieval peasant at a remote village; traverse a beautiful and ancient landscape while revelling in the views of the Lot Valley; enter this fine city across Europe's best preserved fortified medieval bridge; and scurry along narrow corridors to a magnificent cathedral (Walk 12). Similar experiences await you throughout France. You can use a car and public transportation or, if you do not rent a car, use only public transportation to reach starting and ending points. Specific directions are included in the final section for each walk.

Introduction

In order to plan a remarkable tour of France, consult the map on page 9, and look at the suggested itineraries listed below. For travellers with time to burn, there is a comprehensive itinerary, the Grand Tour, which combines all of the greatest sites with a collection of France's best walks. The Grand Tour is peerless as a vehicle for an in-depth discovery of France.

There are also four regional itineraries: Paris and Vicinity (especially useful for those with only a few days to spend in France); Normandy, Brittany, and the Loire Valley; the South of France; and France: the East.

Another unique feature of this book is the inclusion of eleven thematic tours: Famous Cathedrals, Churches, and Basilicas; Castle Walks; Ocean and Sea; Medieval World; Inland Waterways; High Hills and Massive Mountains; Art Walks; Forgotten Abbeys; Fabulous Forests; Must-See Itinerary: All the Most Famous Sights; and Author's Favorite Walks.

Although there is a remarkable diversity of tours available to select from, do not consider this to be a straight-jacket. Feel free to construct your own itinerary or combine two or more of the suggested itineraries. In order to determine which particular walks are most attractive for you, inspect the Walks-At-A-Glance section on pages 22–36, which provides capsule summaries of each adventure.

Itineraries

The following diverse itineraries are suggested, but feel free to construct your own by using the maps and walk summaries.

Grand Tour

For the finest tour available in all of France, complete all of the walks in the order presented (1–35), which is achieved by completing each of the following regional itineraries. An ambitious, fast-driving traveller could do them all in less than seven weeks, including ten days in Paris. For a less frenetic tour, budget about nine or ten weeks. For more details, simply follow the sequence of the four regional itineraries.

Regional Itineraries

The itineraries are given here in their most compressed form. If you are not on a tight schedule, feel free to intersperse your walks with free days to explore each region in more depth or simply to relax. Also, on one-night stops you may not arrive in time to make a required public transportation rendezvous, necessitating an extra day in town; or you may not feel like getting out of your car and going immediately on a walk. Be judicious with available time, and do not push yourself too hard. Remember, you are on vacation. On the other hand it usually is possible for tireless travellers to adhere to the suggested itineraries and enjoy the fast-paced succession of sites and walks. The suggested travel routes are simply the fastest (remember, routes designated "A" or "autoroute" are toll roads, while all other roads are free) or most direct. Please ignore them, if you have the time, and create a more interesting route along France's beautiful back roads. These itineraries, which take you to a variety of off-the-beaten-path locations, are slightly more difficult via public transportation and may involve convoluted routing in order to reach some destinations. However, for the patient traveller it is possible to arrive at all of the destinations, and I have indicated whether it is possible to reach a destination by train or if a train/bus combination is required. You can get detailed information on connections at any train station and can plan your entire itinerary from Paris, or you can make use of the detailed public transportation information available in one of the more general travel guides to France, such as the *Let's Go* series. Finally, the suggestions about where to stay can easily be altered to suit your needs; however, they are generally the most attractive alternative in a given area. I have included a few specific lodging recommendations, but the tourist office, a quick ride

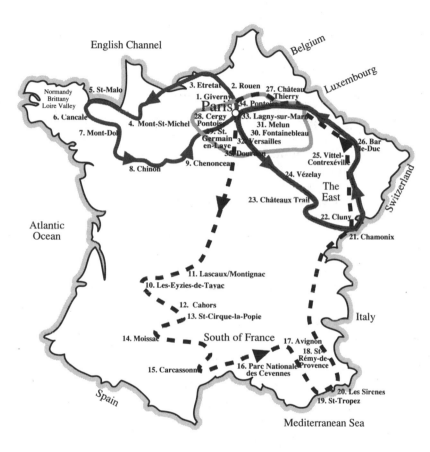

English Channel

Belgium

Luxembourg

Normandy
Brittany
Loire Valley

5. St-Malo

3. Etretat   2. Rouen   27. Château
1. Giverny   Thierry
Paris   34. Pontoise

6. Cancale

4. Mont-St-Michel   28. Cergy   33. Lagny-sur-Marne
Pontoise   31. Melun

7. Mont-Dol   29. St.   30. Fontainebleau
Germain   32. Versailles
en-Laye   35. Dourdan   26. Bar
le-Duc

25. Vittel-
Contrexéville

8. Chinon   9. Chenonceau

24. Vézelay   The
East

23. Châteaux Trail

Switzerland

Atlantic
Ocean

22. Cluny

21. Chamonix

11. Lascaux/Montignac

10. Les-Eyzies-de-Tayac

12. Cahors

13. St-Cirque-la-Popie

Italy

14. Moissac   South of France   17. Avignon

18. St-
Rémy-de-
Provence

15. Carcassonne   16. Parc Nationale
des Cevennes

Spain

20. Les Sirenes
19. St-Tropez

Mediterranean Sea

around town (prices are always visible on the exterior of French hotels), or a comprehensive guidebook that specializes in lodging will provide you with a more in-depth overview of the local accommodation scene. Rooms are seldom difficult to find in France, especially if you are in a car. However, if you are relying on public transportation, you may wish to consult a guide book and reserve hotel rooms in advance.

1. Normandy, Brittany, and the Loire Valley

This itinerary includes many of the greatest and most accessible sights in France. Visitors with time constraints will enjoy this tour, which involves a minimal amount of driving or time on public transportation.

Nights 1–3: Rouen (Walks 1 and 2)
From Paris drive eighty miles (along A13; or train from Paris' Gare St-Lazare) to Rouen, where there are numerous accommodations in and around the city. Several American-style Hôtel Campaniles ring the city and allow easy parking at your door. Other suburban-type hotels, all in the moderate price range, beckon. Spend three nights here. Tour Rouen the first night and do Walks 1 (Vernon to Giverny) and 2 (La Fontaine to Saint-Martin-de-Boscherville) on the following two days.

Night 4: Etretat (Walk 3)
A short hop from Rouen (N15 to D926 to Fecamp, then D940 to Etretat; or frequent trains from Rouen) takes you to Etretat, where there are numerous accommodations. Find a room, do Walk 3 (Vattetot-sur-Mer to Etretat), enjoy sandy beaches, and savor a beautiful sunset.

Nights 5–9: Saint-Malo (Walks 4–7)
Saint-Malo (about five hours drive from Etretat: D139 and D925 to Le Havre, A15 and A13 to Caen, N175 to Pontorson, D797 and D155 to Saint-Malo; or trains from Etretat), with its numerous accommodations and ample parking just beyond the city gates, is an

excellent base for exploring Brittany's wild coastline. Spend night five exploring the town and plan Walks 4 (Courtils to Mont-Saint-Michel), 5 (St-Lunaire to St-Malo), 6 (Pointe de Grouin to Cancale), and 7 (Vivier-sur-Mer to Dol-de-Bretagne) for the next four days. Or if you prefer, you may wish to spend a night at Mont-Saint-Michel, Dol-de-Bretagne, or Cancale, all worthy of your time.

Nights 10–12: Amboise (Walks 8 and 9)

Amboise, just east of Tours, is about five hours drive from Saint-Malo (N137 to Rennes, N157 and A81 to Le Mans, N138 to Tours, D751 to Amboise; or trains from Saint-Malo). Although not one of our walking destinations, Amboise, with its adequate accommodations and convenient location, is an excellent base for touring the Loire Valley. Spend the first day in Amboise exploring the famous fortified *château* and the home of Leonardo da Vinci. The next two days can be spent pursuing Walks 8 (Hôpital Saint-Benoit-la-Forêt to Château de Chinon) and 9 (La Croix-en-Touraine to Château de Chenonceau). The return to Paris from Amboise (D31 to A10) is only about two hours of easy expressway driving or a short train trip.

2. *The South of France*

This longest tour encompasses many of France's greatest sites, while taking you through the sun-drenched Provençal back country and along the ethereal beauty of the Mediterranean coast.

Nights 1–3: Montignac or Sarlat-la-Canéda (Walks 10 and 11)

A long day's drive from Paris (autoroute A10 from Paris to Orléans, then autoroute A71 to Clermont-Ferrand, where you take N89 just past Brive-la-Gaillard, turning south on D60 to Sarlat; or by train to Brive-la-Gaillard and then bus to Montignac or by train to Sarlat) will take you to Montignac and the prehistoric caves of Lascaux. Spend the first night at Montignac recovering from the harrowing road experience and complete Walks 10 (Le Bugue to Les Eyzies—about 15 miles southeast of Montignac) and 11 (Route de

Saint-Amand-de-Coly to Montignac) over the next two days. Another excellent lodging alternative is Sarlat-la-Canéda, which is less than twenty miles from both walks. This wonderfully preserved medieval town offers numerous accommodations and is a visual delight.

Nights 4–5: Cahors (Walks 12 and 13)

Cahors is an easy $1\frac{1}{2}$-hour drive from Sarlat (D704 to N20; or by train). There are hotels in most price ranges within the town and several chain hotels just north of the city. The Hôtel de France, almost directly across from the train station, offers very attractive, modern rooms at reasonable prices; and one of the finest vegetarian restaurants in France, l'Orangerie, can be found in the medieval quarter. Arrive in town, book a room, and take the short Walk 13 to St-Cirque-la-Popie, leaving plenty of time to wander narrow medieval corridors at night. The next day, take the superb Walk 12 from Douelle to Cahors.

Night 6: Moissac (Walk 14)

About $1\frac{1}{2}$ hours southwest of Cahors (D653, D953, and D957; or by train) along attractive back roads lies medieval Moissac, where the abbey harbors one of the most beautiful cloisters in Europe. Check into a hotel (there are several, in a variety of price ranges), take eventful Walk 14 (Castelsarrasin to Moissac) down a beautiful canal, and pass the afternoon exploring the town and *abbaye*.

Nights 7–8: Carcassonne (Walk 15)

A $1\frac{1}{2}$-hour drive southwest from Moissac along the ultra-fast autoroute Deux Mers (A61; or by train) takes you to fantasy-castle Carcassonne. There are numerous accommodations at all price ranges here; for the most convenience, try one of the moderately-priced hotels that offer free parking just across from the main gate. Spend the first day exploring the castle and town or just relaxing in scenic splendor. On the next day, take Walk 15 (Conques-sur-Orbeil to Carcassonne) and enjoy superb views of the castle from the distance.

Nights 8–9: Villefort (Parc National des Cevennes) (Walk 16)

About 200 miles or 4 hours from Carcassonne lies remote Villefort (A9 to Nîmes, N106 to Alès, D906 to Villefort; or by train), which is attractively situated in a deep, verdant valley and has an adequate number of hotels and restaurants. The Hôtel-Restaurant du Lac about a mile north of town offers attractive, moderately-priced lake-view rooms and a slightly expensive but high-quality restaurant with panoramic lake views. Spend the first day lounging, engaging in outdoor sports, or exploring this beautiful region. On day two take the long Walk 16 (Gare de Prévenchères to Villefort).

Nights 10–12: Avignon (Walks 17 and 18)

Avignon (about three hours of winding roads along D906, to Alès, and D981 and N100 to Avignon; or by train) has numerous accommodations both within the walls and clustering along autoroute exits just north and south of the city. Given the difficult parking situation within the walls, I tend to stay in the suburbs. However, if this is your first trip to Avignon, it may be worth the parking hassle to stay within the walls and savor this beautiful city. Spend the first day wandering about this lively living museum while revelling in the sophisticated street life. The next two days will take you from worldly Avignon into the serene beauty of the Provençal back country as you complete Walks 17 (Roquemaure to Villeneuve-les-Avignon/Avignon) and 18 (Les Baux to St-Remy-de-Provence).

Nights 13–15: Côte d'Azur—Saint-Tropez (Walks 19 and 20)

About $2\frac{1}{2}$ hours from the urbanity of Avignon (A7 and A8 to D25, and N98 and D98a to Saint-Tropez; or train to Saint-Raphael and bus to Saint-Tropez) lies the sensuous Mediterranean seacoast known as the Côte d'Azur. Hotels, in all price ranges, are ubiquitous throughout the entire coastal region. However, less-expensive lodging is increasingly difficult to find, and during the summer, when almost the entire French population is gathered en masse for fun and traffic jams, any room can be difficult to find. Be persistent, and you will eventually find a room somewhere along the coast. Spend the first day looking for a room and enjoying the resort ambience. The next two days, delight in walking away from the crowds with Walks 19 (Plage de Pampelonne to Saint-Tropez) and 20 (Les Sirènes to Saint-Aygulf).

3. France: The East

With the exception of Chamonix, this area of France is not over-run with tourists and offers an attractive package of off-the-beaten-path sights. The tour starts in Chamonix, which allows you to do the lion's share of driving or train riding on the first day, assuring a more leisurely return to Paris.

Nights 1–2: Chamonix (Walk 21)
About $6^{1}/_{2}$ hours from Paris (A6 to Macon then A40 to Chamonix; or several trains per day from Paris) lies imposing Mont-Blanc, Europe's tallest mountain, and its most picturesque village, Chamonix. The tourist office is most accommodating here and will find you lodging in one the town's numerous hotels; or you may simply wander around until you find a suitable place to spend the night. During the summer there are always rooms available. Spend the first night walking about and enjoying the mountain ambience after a long drive. Day two, enjoy Walk 21 (Argentière to Chamonix) along the valley floor. Day three, pick up a local map and explore the heights via cable cars. Everywhere you go the views are spectacular.

Night 3: Cluny (Walk 22)
About three hours drive (A40 to Macon then N79 and D981 to Cluny; or train to Macon and S.N.C.F. bus to Cluny) from Chamonix lies remote Cluny and its abbey, former queen of medieval splendor. Start early, arrive before noon, book a room (the tourist office will help you with accommodations, or try the reasonably-priced Hôtel du Commerce on the main street; if for some reason the town is crowded, stay at Macon about 15 miles east), take the

short Walk 22 (Lournand to Cluny), visit the abbey, and enjoy an evening in this tranquil town.

Night 4: Arbois (Walk 23)

A scenic two-hour drive from Cluny (D981 to Cormatin, D14 to Tournus, D975, D971, and N78 to Lons-le-Saunier, and N83 to Arbois; or bus to Macon and train to Arbois) will take you to Arbois, one of the most attractive small towns in the Jura, where there are a variety of accommodations. You may also try Salins-les-Bains, known for its hot-spring resorts, just north of Arbois. (Note: there is also an excellent but difficult walk between these two towns; see "Suggestions for More Walking" under Walk 23). Check into a hotel, take Walk 23 (Château Trail, just south of Arbois and along the same rail line) and enjoy an evening in this valley paradise. Do not forget to try the fine and unusual yellow Arbois wines.

Night 5: Vézelay (Walk 24)

From Arbois to Vézelay is about three hours (D469 to Mont-St-Vaudrey, N5 and D405 to Dole, A36 to Beaune, A6 to Avallon, and D957 to Vézelay; or several trains to Sermizelles and then bus to Vézelay). There are several hotels in Vézelay that are usually not fully occupied, but it is also possible to spend the night at attractive Avallon only about ten miles from Vézelay. Check into a hotel, take Walk 24 (Asquins to Vézelay), tour the Basilica, and enjoy a fine meal accompanied by excellent, locally-grown Burgundy wines.

Night 6: Contrexéville/Vittel (Walk 25)

A mostly expressway ride from Vézelay to Contrexéville or Vittel (D957 to Avallon, A6 to Beaune, A31 to D164 to Contrexéville or Vittel; or bus to Sermizelles and trains to Contrexéville or Vittel) will take only about three hours. There are numerous accommodations in most price ranges in both attractive towns. Check into a hotel, take Walk 25 (Contrexéville to Vittel), and enjoy the spas and casinos. You may be seduced into an extra evening.

Night 7: Bar-le-Duc (Walk 26)

A quick two-hour drive from Contrexéville/Vittel to Bar-le-Duc along a series of primarily back roads (D164 to Domremy, D966 to Ligny-en-Barrois, and N135 to Bar-le-Duc; or by train) will land you in a most attractive historical city. Lodging should not be difficult to find, and the hotel directly across from the train station has very nice, recently-remodelled rooms for a moderate price. After finding a room, take Walk 26 (Trémont-sur-Sault to Bar-le-Duc), and tour the town.

Night 8: Château-Thierry (Walk 27)

Château-Thierry is only about two hours by car from Bar-le-Duc (N35 to A4 to Château-Thierry; or by train). There are several hotels in town or stay near the expressway at the comfortable Hôtel Campanile. Enjoy Walk 27 (Chezy-sur-Marne to Château-Thierry), visit the town, and return to Paris on the next morning (about $1^1/_2$ hours on A4).

4. Paris and Vicinity (Walks 28–35)

Excellent public transportation from Paris to the rest of France makes these walks possible as short day trips. Hotels are omnipresent throughout Paris, and the tourist offices at the airports and train stations can book rooms for you. I have stayed several times at the Hôtel Carofftel Gobelins (18, avenue des Gobelins, 75005 Paris; tel. (33–1) 45 35 80 12) in the fifth arrondissement, which is a quick walk to the rue de Mouffetard with its numerous restaurants and lively nightlife, and only about twenty minutes to the Latin Quarter. (Also, just around the corner on the rue Pascale is the Bol-en-Bois, Paris's most venerable vegetarian restaurant). This small, comfortable, and friendly two-star hotel is owned by sisters Christine and Chantale, who speak English and are very helpful in any matter related to your stay in Paris. Specific directions for the completion of the following walks from your base in Paris are given in the final section of this book:

Thematic Itineraries

To plan a thematic itinerary, refer to the regional itineraries and select the relevant portions. For example, if you were to select the Famous Cathedrals, Churches, and Basilicas thematic tour, you would refer to the Normandy, Brittany, and Loire Valley regional itinerary for directions on Walks 1–3; the South of France itinerary for Walks 12, 15, and 17; France: the East for Walks 24 and 26; and the Paris itinerary for Walk 34. In addition to the following itineraries, you may customize any itinerary using the same procedure.

1. Famous Cathedrals, Churches, and Basilicas

France has many beautiful and renowned cathedrals, churches, and basilicas. The following walks terminate or originate at one of them:

1. Vernon to Giverny
2. Rouen: La Fontaine to Saint-Martin-de-Boscherville
3. Vivier-sur-Mer to Dol-de-Bretagne
12. Douelle to Cahors
15. Conques-sur-Orbeil to Carcassonne
17. Roquemaure to Villeneuve-les-Avignon (Avignon)
24. Asquins to Vézelay
26. Trémont-sur-Sault to Bar-le-Duc
34. Pontoise to Auvers-sur-Oise

2. Castle Walks

France is the home of chivalry and knighthood. This is reflected in the great castles that are found throughout the country. For a visit to France's finest fortifications, try the following walks:

8. Hôpital Saint-Benoit-la-Forêt to Château de Chinon
9. La Croix-en-Touraine to Château de Chenonceau
12. Conques-sur-Orbeil to Carcassone
17. Roquemaure to Villeneuve-les-Avignon (Avignon)
18. Les Baux-de-Provence to St-Remy-de-Provence
23. Château Trail
27. Chézy-sur-Marne to Château-Thierry
29. Saint-Germain-en-Laye to Maisons-Laffitte
30. Fountainebleau to Bois-le-Rois
32. Versailles to Saint-Cyr-l'Ecole
35. Sermaise to Dourdan

3. Ocean and Sea

The following walks take full advantage of France's stunningly beautiful coastal scenery:

3. Vattetot-sur-Mer to Etretat
4. Courtils to Mont-Saint-Michel
5. St-Lunaire to St-Malo
6. Pointe de Grouin to Cancale
7. Vivier-sur-Mer to Dol-de-Bretagne
19. Plage de Pampelonne to Saint-Tropez
20. Les Sirènes to Saint-Aygulf

4. Medieval World

Remnants of the medieval world are ubiquitous throughout France, and the following walks will transport you back into the life of the Middle Ages:

5. Inland Waterways

The following walks follow, at least partially, the course of France's beautiful lakes, rivers, and canals:

6. High Hills and Massive Mountains

Although not necessarily too strenuous, the following walks involve at least one good climb or capture the scenic splendor of

France's mountains and hills:

   7. Vivier-sur-Mer to Dol-de-Bretagne
10. Le Bugue to Les Eyzies
16. Gare de Prévenchères to Villefort
17. Roquemaure to Villeneuve-les-Avignon (Avignon)
18. Les Baux-de-Provence to St-Rémy-de-Provence
21. Argentière to Chamonix
24. Asquins to Vézelay
27. Chézy-sur-Marne to Château-Thierry
35. Sermaise to Dourdan

7. Art Walks

The following walks take you to the sites painted by great artists:

   1. Vernon to Giverny
   2. Rouen: La Fontaine to Saint-Martin-de-Boscherville
   3. Vattetot-sur-Mer to Etretat
18. Les Baux-de-Provence to St-Rémy-de-Provence
34. Pontoise to Auvers-sur-Oise

8. Forgotten Abbeys

The haunting loneliness and pacific tranquility of the Middle Ages is most easily evoked at an abandoned abbey. The following walks will take you into these treasures of the past and back to the Middle Ages:

   2. Rouen: La Fontaine to Saint-Martin-de-Boscherville
   4. Courtils to Mont-Saint-Michel
14. Castelsarrasin to Moissac
17. Roquemaure to Villeneuve-les-Avignon (Avignon)
22. Lournand to Cluny

9. Fabulous Forests

France is renowned for the beauty of its forests, and the following walks will transport you into a world of leafy solitude:

2. Rouen: La Fontaine to Saint-Martin-de-Boscherville
8. Hôpital Saint-Benoit-la-Forêt to Château de Chinon
9. La Croix-en-Touraine to Château de Chenonceau
11. Route de St-Amand-de-Coly to Lascaux/Montignac
18. Les Baux-de-Provence to St-Rémy-de-Provence
21. Argentière to Chamonix
23. Château Trail
25. Contrexéville to Vittel
27. Chézy-sur-Marne to Château-Thierry
29. Saint-Germain-en-Laye to Maisons-Laffitte
30. Fountainebleau to Bois-le-Rois
32. Versailles to Saint-Cyr-l'Ecole

10. Must-See Itinerary: All the Greatest Sights

If you have limited time in France, and wish to see the most famous sites while enjoying a great walk, choose from among the following:

3. Vattetot-sur-Mer to Etretat
4. Courtils to Mont-Saint-Michel
9. La Croix-en-Touraine to Château de Chenonceau
11. Route de St-Amand-de-Coly to Lascaux/Montignac
12. Douelle to Cahors
15. Conques-sur-Orbeil to Carcassonne
17. Roquemaure to Villeneuve-les-Avignon (Avignon)
19. Plage de Pampelonne to Saint-Tropez
21. Argentière to Chamonix
24. Asquins to Vézelay
30. Fontainebleau to Bois-le-Rois
32. Versailles to Saint-Cyr-l'Ecole

11. Author's Favorite Walks

The following walks were difficult to select, and they may not include the most famous sights, but in each case the walk itself is superb:

3. Vattetot-sur-Mer to Etretat
7. Vivier-sur-Mer to Dol-de-Bretagne
10. Le Bugue to Les Eyzies
16. Gare de Prévenchères to Villefort
19. Plage de Pampelonne to Saint-Tropez
21. Argentière to Chamonix
23. Château Trail
28. Cergy-Pontoise
25. Sermaise to Dourdan

Walks-at-a-Glance

These brief summaries will help you decide which itinerary is best for you or allow you to assemble your own unique itinerary. Full details for each walk can be found in Section Two.

Walk 1   *Monet's Water Lilies:* Vernon to Giverny

This is a great walk between two outstanding towns. Vernon is an accommodating, riverine patch of urbanity where Monet began painting churches and where you will perhaps pass an enchanting evening. Leaving Vernon, you will follow a rails-to-trails path that includes partially-exposed railway ties and enjoy excellent views of the Seine and Vernon as you whistle-stop your way to the water lilies. Soon you will climb into an emerald green forest known by Monet and essentially unchanged by encroaching civilization. Finally, you will descend quickly into Giverny entering Monet's home and his private, water-lily world. A fantastic three miles.

Walk 2   ***Rouen:*** *La Fontaine to Saint-Martin-de-Boscherville*

Rouen, with its Gothic masterpieces (Monet painted cathedrals here) and magnificent neighborhoods lined with carefully restored, timbered homes, is one of France's most attractive large cities. A short bus ride away from this urban magnificence, the twelfth-century, Romanesque jewel Abbaye St-Georges in St-Martin-de-Boscherville lies recumbent in bucolic serenity. En route to the abbey, you will ascend from the diminutive, riverside La Fontaine and be greeted by expansive views of the Seine River valley. Soon the views become partially occluded as you walk high among dense stands of forest. The forest cedes to marvellous views of the abbey as you approach majestically medieval Saint-Martin from lofty cliffs lining the lovely Seine.

Walk 3   ***Normandy:*** *Vattetot-sur-Mer to Etretat*

A short, but unforgettable, excursion from Rouen or Honfleur to the Atlantic coast of Normandy will bring you to the famous cliffs of Etretat. The cliffs—painted by numerous artists, including Monet, Courbet, and Boudin—soar over two hundred feet and provide some of the most spectacular walking scenery available anywhere. You will spend almost the entire walk along the white cliffs of the Atlantic Ocean. On a clear day you will be able to see far into the ocean, experience great views of the cliffs, and spy sunbathers on remote beaches far below. The sounds of ocean, wind, and sea gulls will be your constant companions.

Walk 4   *Courtils to Mont-Saint-Michel*

Truly one of the world's great sites, the abbey church of Mont-Saint-Michel soars high above a precipitous, unadorned rock that becomes an island when it is enveloped by the fast flowing evening tide. Visit the abbey as the culmination of today's pilgrimage, retro-experiencing the trials and tribulations of a medieval voyager. Walking through remote, rustic Courtils and then through a series of seldom used rural tracks, you will soon reach the extensive bay of Mont-Saint-Michel, where you will be delighted by the pilgrim's-eye-view of the abbey's astonishing magnificence.

Walk 5   **Brittany:** *St-Lunaire to St-Malo*
Today's walk follows a serpentine six-mile path along the powerful waters of the Atlantic Ocean. This dazzling day begins at the perfectly-restored St-Malo, a former pirate haven, which was almost completely destroyed during the late stages of World War II. The trail starts at lovely ocean-side St-Lunaire and hugs the coast throughout. Look far into the ocean and enjoy frequent views of your destination, St-Malo, as the ocean-side trail takes you along beaches and cliffs, and occasional WWII bunkers.

Walk 6   **Brittany:** *Cancale to Pointe du Grouin*
Climbing out of this friendly, scenic ocean-side resort, you will observe the fertile oyster beds that stretch for miles into the ocean. Ponder tonight's dinner delights. Along the rocky trail, you will marvel at some of the most rugged coastal scenery on the European continent. Your destination, celebrated Pointe du Grouin, delights with astonishing views of the tempestuous Atlantic and its serrated coast. On a clear day, distant Mont-Saint-Michel can be seen.

Walk 7   ***Brittany:*** *Vivier-sur-Mer to Mont-Dol to Dol-de-Bretagne*

Begin this exciting and eventful walk in a picturesque, ocean-side village where you can marvel at distant Mont-Saint-Michel rising majestically above undulating waves. Head inland along florid country lanes; traverse three picturesque villages; and climb mysterious Mont-Dol, where it is said that the Devil left his claw print while locked in a terrific struggle with the Archangel Michael. Finally, you will saunter quickly into one of France's best preserved and most accommodating medieval towns, Dol-de-Bretagne.

Walk 8   ***Loire Valley:*** *Hôpital Saint-Benoit-le-Forêt to Château de Chinon*

Penetrate an ancient forest where French kings and nobility, riding tall horses, hunted their evening feast; watch France grow before your very eyes as you amble through encroaching suburbs and an architecturally worthy industrial park; approaching Chinon, you will be amazed by numerous *maisons trogolodytes*, which are still-inhabited homes carved into sheer rock; stroll onto the grounds of one of France's most celebrated *châteaux*, where Joan of Arc first encountered the French king; and saunter through the narrow, medieval streets of this most civilized and gracious town. Truly a walk to be savored.

Walk 9   ***Chenonceau:*** *La Croix-en-Touraine to Château de Chenonceau*

Perambulate this riverside path from tranquil, park-like Bléré while skirting encroaching suburban development, traversing fertile fields, and navigating a deep forest. This wonderful jaunt leads you to France's most elegant *château*, celebrated Château de

Chenonceau, which gloriously spans the shimmering, mirror-like Cher River. The views of this masterpiece from the trail are unparalleled and accessible only to the walker.

Walk 10   *Le Bugue to Les Eyzies-de-Tayac*
Walk high in the land of early man on this lengthy but eventful adventure, which begins at lively Le Bugue along the winsome banks of the Vezère River. Traversing fields, forests, and hamlets, you will soon arrive at St-Cirque and visit the famous Grotte (cave) du Sorcier (renowned for its excellent prehistoric drawings) and then encounter the Gorge d'Enfer (Hell's Canyon), a fascinating site of early human habitation. Unforgettable cliff-shaded Les Eyzies, one of the greatest centers of early human discovery, is the home of two excellent museums and is a bustling center for prehistoric cave exploration.

Walk 11   *Route de St-Amand-de-Coly to Lascaux/ Montignac*
Pass almost directly through a working, inhabited *château* sheltered in an expansive, verdant valley; climb high onto a lovely plateau where beautiful vistas abound; and savor verdant, pristine forests as you amble toward Lascaux, which harbors the most famous of all prehistoric cave paintings. Along the way you will come upon the site of Regourdou where, in 1957, the almost complete skeleton of a 70,000-year-old Neanderthal man was found. Finally, find repose at popular Montignac where you can stroll along river banks, wander about narrow lanes, and perhaps rent a canoe or kayak for a float down the Vezère.

Walk 12 *Douelle to Cahors*

Starting at tradition-bound but engaging Douelle where nothing has happened in centuries, you will climb high into the stratosphere amidst remarkable views of the fertile Lot Valley and distant hill country. Distant vistas beckon, and soon you will reach a cliff top worshipped by hang gliders who risk life and limb for a quick glide over the Lot River. As you approach Cahors, through this undulating arcadia, lovely stone fences grace your way and soon you will span the unique and impressive fourteenth-century fortified bridge, Pont Valentré, the best preserved in all of Europe. Explore medieval Cahors along winding narrow streets and imbibe some of the finest wine in France. This uncluttered, architecturally-unique town is one of France's most beautiful.

Walk 13 *Bouzies to St-Cirque-la-Popie to Tour de Faure*

Follow the placid, slow-moving Lot River along grassy river banks shaded by tall cliffs. Leaving the river, you will make a short but precipitous climb to St-Cirque-La-Popie, where expansive views of the Lot and environs startle from the vantage point of a ruined *château* looming 250 feet above the river. Wander narrow streets and marvel at the ancient homes now mostly restored by artists and writers enchanted by the region's ethereal charm. Visit the fifteenth-century church; climb to the formidable Château de Gardette; and relax over an expensive lunch or drink before making the easy descent to wide-spot-in-the-road Tour de Faure where your car or the bus stop is waiting.

Walk 14 *Castelsarrasin to Moissac*

This uniformly lovely, level, and tranquil walk follows

the general route of the most popular of medieval pilgrimages. Departing from amiable Castelsarrasin, you will stroll down a nineteenth-century canal towpath that serves as an extended park for residents along its entire length. People fish, picnic, play games, and jog, cycle, and walk along the path while the canal is a haven for pleasure cruisers. Watch for effusively floral houses that accompany each canal lock and be dumbfounded by the mid-way Motel/Restaurant Felix whose Wild West decor appears to have been inspired by a B-grade Hollywood set designer. Moissac, a stately terminus and a major stop on the medieval pilgrimage trail to Santiago da Compostela, radiates gently from the banks of the Tarn River, providing an intimate frame for the profoundly medieval abbey that provides the focal point and *raison d'être* for this treasure of the Middle Ages.

Walk 15   *Conques-sur-Orbeil to Carcassonne*

Rejoice in the astonishing view of distant Carcassonne as you set out on this medieval trek. It is an experience similar to spying Camelot, or perhaps even Oz (sorry, no yellow brick road to tread upon) in the distance and knowing that great adventure awaits in a remote and mysterious citadel. Carcassonne is the most wonderfully preserved/rebuilt fortress in France, and the walk to this living relic of the Middle Ages retains many startling vistas as you traverse forest, field, vineyard, and river bank to this mystical destination, which was the setting for the recent swashbuckling film *Robin Hood*.

Walk 16   ***Parc National des Cevennes (Land of Robert Louis Stevenson):*** *Gare de Prévenchères to Villefort*

Depart from an abandoned train station that looks like it could be a set for a spaghetti western; climb to a high plateau; amble through an ancient hamlet and around a beautiful blue lake; trek tirelessly along an abandoned "ghost road" that skirts a deep canyon with a fast-flowing river often in view; stride briskly into the still-living, medieval walled-town La Garde Guérin; peregrinate down a medieval pilgrimage/business route, La Voie Régordane; circle another beautiful lake; and arrive in a beautiful hill town just in time for an fulfilling feast. All of this takes place in the land where Robert Louis Stevenson recorded his famous perambulations with a mule in *Travels with a Donkey in the Cevennes.*

Walk 17   ***Provence:*** *Roquemaure to Villeneuve-les-Avignon (Avignon)*

Leaving the leafy languor of Roquemaure, an attractive city built around a number of comely and intimate squares, you will enter an arid, brilliantly-illuminated world that offers a wonderful sequence of astonishing vistas. Traverse bountiful vineyards while contemplating tonight's fine wine; tunnel through densely forested areas that offer welcome respite from intense solar activity; and trek high on a quiet plateau with awesome views of the mountains and valley forming today's dramatic backdrop. Your approach to Villeneuve-les-Avignon will be enhanced by unique views of the mighty, fourteenth-century Fort St-André, which is one of the finest fortifications extant from the Middle Ages. After traversing the length of historic Villeneuve-les-Avignon, you will soon arrive in arty Avignon, walled city of abducted popes, famous for its Palace of the Popes and collapsed bridge Pont St-Bénézet ("Pont d'Avignon" of children's song fame).

Walk 18 **Provence:** *Les Baux-de-Provence to St-Remy-de-Provence*

Les Baux-de-Provence, a most sinister appearing medieval fortress, rises directly out of a rocky promontory that surveys the appropriately named boulder-burdened and burning Val d'Enfer (Hell's Valley). Here brutal masters terrorized the surrounding lands during the Middle Ages and the decadent ruins still stun modern tourists. You will depart from Les Baux and enter into Van Gogh-immortalized landscape along a narrow, rocky trail. The land soon becomes forested and the soon-encountered banks of the man-made Lac de Saint-Rémy offer cool refuge from the midday sun. After tearing yourself from this forested shelter, you will quickly arrive at the ruins of the Roman town of Glanum and the twelfth-century Monastère Saint-Paul de Mausole, where the deeply-disturbed Vincent Van Gogh was treated in 1889 and 1890. After exploring the ruins, complete the walk to broad-boulevarded Saint-Rémy-de-Provence, birthplace of Nostradamus.

Walk 19 **Côte d'Azur:** *Plage de Pampelonne to Saint-Tropez*

Lovers of the human body will linger long at the Plage de Pampelonne, where, during the summer, there are more square inches of flesh than grains of sand. When you begin to suffer from ocular fatigue, start along the littoral-hugging trail to the next dazzling beach. The trail, frequently forested, is punctuated by a variety of large and small beaches. All are topless, and some of the smaller strands are nude. Stop where you feel comfortable, swim, relax, and continue your merry march to Saint-Tropez.

Walk 20 Côte d'Azur: *Les Sirènes to Saint-Aygulf*

Alternating between sandy beach and rugged, rocky pathways, today's trail will take you through crowds of bronzed and lobster-red beach potatoes and onto secluded, seldom visited coastal enclaves. Your walk will end at the pleasant resort of Saint-Aygulf, which has a broad, sandy, and popular beach. Nothing historic here: just the finest beaches and greatest views of the Mediterranean Sea.

Walk 21 Alps: *Argentière to Chamonix*

Walk between two famous mountain towns along an enchanting forest path with stunning views of Mont-Blanc, Europe's tallest mountain, throughout the entire trek. From time to time, tear your eyes from high-mountain panorama and commune with the serenity of the picturesque valley floor: forests, meadows, shallow mountain streams, and the frigid Arve River. In the shadow of Mont-Blanc, Chamonix, your destination and the most ancient of alpine ski villages, is not to be missed.

Walk 22 Lournand to Cluny

Traverse vast fields of golden sunflowers cascading delicately from luminous hilltops—beautiful enough to stop Van Gogh in his tracks, easel and all; walk high along a ridge with excellent vistas of farmlands, vineyards, and forests in this beautiful hill country; enter Cluny along narrow, medieval-looking streets, while examining homes dating back to the twelfth century; inspect the awesome ruins of an abbey that once ruled a vast ecclesiastical empire. This short walk provides a stunning introduction to one of medieval Europe's most important monuments.

Walk 23   *Château Trail:* Passenans to Domblans
This is a wonderfully eventful journey through a captivating countryside. From the remote but still inhabited train station at Passenans you will soon traverse the entire weather-beaten village and pass into a verdant world of forests and vineyards. Along the way to Domblans, you will encounter several *châteaux* and one of the most picturesquely situated churches in France at Frontenay—truly an ethereal vision and one of the most alluring sights on any trail in France. Do not miss this off-the-beaten-path walk in this remote, untouristed region of France.

Walk 24   *Asquins to Vézelay*
Fine wine, rolling green hills, placid rivers, and medieval memories make this area of Burgundy a walker's paradise. From Asquins, a sleepy town ensconced along the banks of the Cure River, you will climb quickly into the congenial rusticity of the surrounding landscape: your destination, the beautiful basilica at Vézelay, remains in glorious view throughout the entire walk. The basilica, according to tradition the final resting place of Mary Magdalene, was one of the Middle Ages' most revered sites. Pilgrims still arrive by the busload, but you will be alone on the trail with all the best views.

Walk 25   *Water Wonderland:* Contrexéville to Vittel
Contrexéville and Vittel are famous names in France and rapidly becoming well known among mineral-water cognoscenti in the United States. The cause of

such robust name recognition is the wonderfully pure mineral waters that emanate from springs in both towns. However, people do not come to these resort towns for a drink of water; they come for the baths,. casinos, elegant ambience, old-world charm, and impressive turn-of-the-century architecture—splendid hotels, public buildings, and ornate grounds abound. A lovely, often wooded trail over rolling hills links these two valley resorts and provides a wonderful contrast between France's past, present, and future—enjoy rustic gentility and genial trails while viewing encroaching shopping malls.

Walk 26   *Trémont-sur-Sault to Bar-le-Duc*

Pass from bucolic "little Venice," Trémont-sur-Sault (fast flowing springs force many residents to construct diminutive bridges to the main street), where you are light years from the tourist France and into an ethereal arcadia replete with dense forests, halcyon hamlets, and undulating fields that bear an eerie resemblance to Andrew Wyeth's signature painting *Christina's World*. Your destination, Bar-le-Duc, beckons with its unspoiled, untouristed but highly alluring medieval ambience. Visit the gothic Eglise Saint-Etienne where you will be terrified by the sixteenth-century *squellette* (skeleton) called "Le Transi"; stroll among fifteenth-century homes lining Place Saint-Pierre; and trace the course of the beautiful Ornain River as it bisects the town.

Walk 27   *Chézy-sur-Marne to Château-Thierry*

Chézy-sur-Marne is a picturesque post-card of a town that has slumbered, with nineteenth-century grace, into the very late twentieth century. Not far from Chézy, you will enter a quiet, sun-drenched world of champagne grapes—some of the finest anywhere. Walking high above the valley floor and occasionally passing through lovely villages, you will see the graceful waters of the Marne River flow languidly through rich, vine-covered fields. You will also visit an impressive monument honoring the Americans who fought to defend France during World War I. Descending from the monument, you will stride comfortably into elegant and historic Château-Thierry, which radiates from the banks of the beautiful Marne River.

Walk 28 *La Ville Nouvelle: Cergy-Préfecture to Cergy-St-Christophe*
From the RER stop at Cergy-Préfecture ascend via escalator to the quiet, car-less town above. This totally planned community should be a model for all cities of the future—everything is on a human scale and built with people, not cars, in mind. Follow the course of the beautiful Oise River, where fishermen phlegmatically cast slow moving flies along the winsome banks and pleasure cruisers float slowly down a serpentine path; make your way up the Axe Majeur, an extensive system of monuments and striking buildings whose assemblage forms an enormous work of outdoor art; and stride in amazement to another planned, architecturally striking community, Cergy-St-Christophe, which also follows the principle of separating cars and people.

Walk 29 *Paris: Saint-Germain-en-Laye to Maisons-Laffitte*
Saint-Germain-en-Laye will be on your short list of must-see sites around Paris. The famous twelfth-century *château* housing a superb museum of prehistoric objects

is the main attraction. After visiting the *château*, you will stroll along the Grande Terrasse, which was built under the direction of the master garden designer Le Notre in the seventeenth century and offers outstanding views of Paris. At the end of the Grande Terrasse you will plunge into the emerald-green solitude of the Forêt Domaniale de Saint-Germain-en-Laye. Emerging from the forest, you will enter Maisons-Laffitte, which is home to another venerable *château* constructed early in the reign of Louis XIV.

Walk 30 *Paris:* Fontainebleau to Bois-le-Rois

After Versailles, Fontainebleau is probably the most celebrated *château* in France. The present *château*, constructed during the sixteenth century by François I, has a splendid exterior that is only excelled by the carefully restored rooms that are open to the public. Visit the sometimes crowded *château* and then walk into the renown Forêt de Fontainebleau, where you will leave the crowds behind. This enchanting walk through France's most famous forest will lead you to the town of Bois-le-Rois, which lurks sleepily on the edge of the forest. There is nothing to do here except enjoy the views of the Seine and relax in one of the few cafés.

Walk 31 *Paris:* Bois-le-Rois to Melun

Seldom straying from the shores of the Seine River, you will savor the sight of Bois-le-Rois' elegant riverside homes, while delighting in the Seine's tree-lined banks, flotilla of slow moving barges, and swarms of serene swans. This pleasant riverside stroll leads to Melun, formerly a Roman city, which now radiates from both banks of the Seine. There are no sites of great note here, but Melun is an agreeable lunch-stop town. If you have time, visit the museum, which at one time served as a home to Louis XIV's finance minister, the convicted embezzler Fouquet.

Walk 32   Paris: *Versailles to Saint-Cyr-l'Ecole*
The ostentatious palace of Versailles, built by dictator Louis XIV, is one of France's most-visited historical sites. If you are in Paris, you will pay a worthwhile visit to his palace. However, after standing in line, sometimes for hours, with DROPS, you will be ardent in your desire to walk away from the crowds. Ten minutes from the palace, as you enter the Forêt Domaniale de Versailles, you will have left the other tourists far behind and will be walking calmly through tranquil forests and along shimmering lakes. Departing the forest, feeling much better for having walked, you will enter St-Cyr-l'Ecole, a good place for lunch and a drink, before returning to Paris on the RER train.

Walk 33   Paris: *Lagny-sur-Marne to Esbly*
Lagny-sur-Marne, with its thirteenth-century church and winsome avenues, lies recumbent and remote along the slow-moving Marne River, which you will quickly cross and enter the silence of the non-vehicular world. Paris will be far from your thoughts as you walk through the verdant countryside with the Marne almost always in view. Many antiquated barges converted to recreational use will plod past you at a pace barely faster than you can walk as you stroll pacifically to Esbly, a pleasant terminus for this walk and a suitable place to re-enter twentieth-century Earth.

Walk 34   Paris: *Pontoise to Auvers-sur-Oise*
The walk to Auvers-sur-Oise will be a pilgrimage for students of art history. This picturesque town, which

describes itself as being the "cradle of Impressionism" in its tourist literature, has hosted the artists Daubigny, Cézanne, Pissarro, Rousseau, Vlaminck, and many others. Vincent Van Gogh spent the last months of his life here and is buried in the town cemetery. The walk from Pontoise, also a favorite Impressionist hang out, is splendid as it courses along the Oise River and through the hamlets, farms, and wheat fields that have been immortalized by many great artists.

Walk 35 *Paris: Sermaise to Dourdan*

Sermaise is a quiet, flowery little village hidden from urban perils near the Orge River about thirty miles from Paris. This part of the Ile-de-France, not yet disfigured by crowds of tourists, has maintained its traditional lifestyles and appearances. The route to Dourdan is a delightful trek through leafy forests, gentle hills, fertile fields, and serene hamlets. Dourdan, with its heavily fortified, well-preserved thirteenth-century *château*, extensive town walls, and impressively large twelfth-century church, serves as this superb walk's worthy culmination.

Part One
Hitting the Trail

1. Before You Leave

Other Travel Guides

The stolidly written but very useful green Michelin Guides provide a good general overview of France. There is a single book that covers all of France and also numerous regional guides. Each has a map in the front that rates the importance of all the sites, major and minor, within a certain region. They also have sections relating to history, culture, and specific monuments. I am often surprised to find even the most obscure places mentioned and do not hesitate to consult these guides when I am formulating walking and driving routes. They can be purchased in many American and European bookstores and are moderately priced.

When my wife purchased a *Let's Go: Europe* book in 1985, I humored her by saying that it was a good idea. What I actually thought was that it was a waste of money, and I had nothing to learn from a cabal of callow college students. Before going to Europe that summer I deigned to regard only the book's cover, shunning the contents. Slowly, while driving, as my wife continued to stridently bark out many useful bits of information, I was converted. At first I would steal glances at a page or two; later I found myself reading whole chapters. Now I would consider no trip without a copy. When I read one of these volumes, I want to leap from my couch, strap on a backpack, throw away (or perhaps just hide) my credit cards, and travel cheaply to all of these wonderful and charming places. I highly recommend purchasing *Let's Go: France* (New York: St. Martin's Press, annual). I have seen no other guide that contains so much information on train/bus schedules, tourist offices, places to change money, laundromats, restaurants, and much more.

I would also recommend the various guides published by Arthur

Frommer, especially if you are looking for more upscale dining and accommodations. However, as I will soon discuss, finding lodging in France is absolutely no problem, and purchasing a book simply for listings of lodgings is not necessary.

For fascinating overviews of the history of France and Paris as it relates to the modern traveller, I strongly recommend Interlink Publishing's *A Traveller's History of France* and *A Traveller's History of Paris*. Each volume offers a complete and authoritative history from the earliest of times up to the present day. A gazetteer cross-referenced to the main text pinpoints the historical importance of many of the sights and towns you will encounter on your walks.

Until I read Colin Fletcher's *Complete Walker*, my few desultory attempts at backpacking and wilderness walking were singularly unsuccessful. This book changed my walking life and made me a successful outdoorsperson. Even if you are only contemplating a walk through a city park, you will probably find some useful tips: every conceivable topic is exhaustively treated. I recommend this book for backpackers and day hikers. Wonderfully written in idiosyncratic "old codger" prose, the *Complete Walker III* (New York: Alfred A. Knopf, 1986) should be found in every walker's bookcase.

Optional Maps and Guides Related to Walking in France

You may wish to purchase a "topo-guide" (*guide topographique*) or map(s) to aid you in the completion of the walks listed in this book, especially if you plan to do extra walking in a particular region. A topo-guide is a written description of the trail with accompanying maps. They are usually about 70 to 150 pages in length, have numerous maps, and cost about $11–15/£7–10. Unfortunately, for most English-speakers, they are written in French. However, I usually rely only on the map for information about the trail and find the written description to be superfluous. The only time I use the written description is when the trail is poorly marked and I am confused. However, in Part Two, I have included detailed trail notes and a map that are designed to help you when problems arise. For each of the walks listed in Part Two, the optional topo-guide and/or maps are listed. The topo-guides are published by Federation Française de la Randonnée Pédestre (FFRP), which is a national organization devoted to creating and maintaining trails, coordinating the activities of regional walking organizations, protecting the environment, and publishing information about the more than 25,000 miles of trails they maintain. The topo-guides can be easily obtained in Paris at their information center at 64, rue de Gergovie, 75014 Paris (telephone: (1) 45 45 31 02). They can also be purchased at Au Vieux Campeur, 3, rue du Sommerand in the fifth arrondissement. For mail order: 48, rue des Ecoles, 75008 Paris (telephone: (1) 60 11 63 62). Both assure me that there is usually a staff member who speaks English. Au Vieux Campeur has most of the necessary maps, or you can obtain them directly from the Institut Géographique Nationale store at 107, rue la Boétie, 75009 Paris (telephone: (1) 42 25 87 90). If you desire the certainty of finding someone who speaks English, call the London bookstore Edward Standford Ltd. (0171–836–1321), where you can order most of the maps and guides that I have listed in Part Two. If they do not have particular items in stock, they will order them for you.

Some of the topo-guides have been translated into English in a series called "Footpaths of Europe." They cost $19.95 each (about £12), and can be ordered in the U.S. from Seven Hills Book Distributors at 1–800–545–2005. Ask for a copy of their free catalogue, which lists many imported books relating to travel. These guides combine walks from several topo-guides into a single book and are accurately translated. I own several of these books, but I prefer the original French topo-guides. I find the English translations to be bulky in comparison, and they have also excluded the important topo-guide information that is summarized in table form relating to distances between towns and the availability of public transportation, lodging, and restaurants. The advantage of having an English translation is slight since I seldom use the trail description. However, if you do not read French you may feel more secure with the English version. In Part Two I have noted English translations when I am aware of them.

The Institut Géographique Nationale (IGN) publishes numerous maps in a variety of scales. Since the topo-guides include IGN 1:50,000 maps (1 cm=0.5 kilometers or 1 $^1/_4$ inches = 1 mile), you will probably wish to purchase a Série Vert (green—meaning the map number appears in a green box on the cover) IGN 1:100,000 map (1 cm=1 kilometer or 1 $^1/_4$ inches=2 miles) of the general area (about \$4–5/£2.50–3.25). The route of the walk will usually appear on these maps, and they are useful if you are driving to your walk, touring the general area, or are prone to straying off the trail. The highly detailed Série Bleu 1:25,000 IGN maps (1 cm=0.25 kilometers or 2 $\frac{1}{2}$ inches=1 mile) are expensive (almost \$10/£6.50) and cover a very limited area. However, they are excellent and very helpful in keeping you from straying from the trail. None of the walks presented in this book requires the use of these maps, but I highly recommend purchasing them.

Language: How Much Is Enough?

Although I read French well and speak it more fluently than most Spanish cows, I sometimes have difficulty understanding what people are saying to me. French is a difficult language to speak and even more difficult to understand. Unlike Germans and Italians, who generally pronounce words as they are written with pauses in between, the French insist on dropping some syllables and running many words together without interruption. Achieving perfect speech and comprehension is generally unattainable unless you are a specialist in the language and spend much time studying in an immersion environment.

Fortunately, fluency in French is not an important factor for a successful walking tour of France, particularly if you enjoy being lost and unable to communicate with anyone. Actually, since there is usually no one around to interrogate, I can think of no instance where language ability would have meant the difference between being lost or found. Furthermore, if you follow the trail notes contained in this book you should have few problems.

However, since few French speak English, you should attempt to learn the language of your host country. If you are like me and cannot afford a private tutor, the next best technique is to purchase language tapes that are packaged with workbooks. The best material I have found is in Passport Books' *Just Listen and Learn* series.

Level of Fitness

If you are already a regular walker, you should have no problem with any of the walks listed in this book. None of the walks require any serious climbing, but a few involve a number of breathtaking ups and downs. In the trail notes, I have listed the approximate amount of climbing that you will do on each trail. If you are not a frequent walker and not involved in an exercise program, you should begin walking regularly a couple of months before you arrive in France. The walks that I have included vary from about two to nine miles, with most ranging from three to six miles. If you can walk four to five miles before you leave, you should be able to complete all of the walks I have listed. There are a number of books that show you how to develop a walking-fitness program. I have never been able to read more than a few pages of such books and find it odd that so much ink has been devoted to such a simple and natural motion. I just begin with a few three-to-five-mile walks and increase the distance until I reach the maximum length of walk that I anticipate completing. At this level of walking fitness, I adjust quickly to walking in France.

Car Rental

If you have decided to drive, you should reserve a car before you leave for France. Renting a car once you have arrived in France is substantially more expensive. I always find the cheapest and most fuel-efficient vehicle: for up to three people who are not large and do not bring much luggage, the smallest vehicles are sufficient. It is best to comparison shop for rates, but I have always found Kemwel to be the least expensive on a long-term basis. The longer you use the car the better the price, and if you lease for a minimum of three weeks you will be able to secure good terms. You can order Kemwel's brochures in the U.S. at 1–800–678–0678. Ask for both the car-rental and car-lease brochures.

Hotel Reservations

I usually reserve a room for my stay in Paris, but it is almost always possible to find a room through the reservation service at the airports and train stations. If you feel insecure without prior reservations, check the listings in the guides I have recommended. I do not like to be too precise about when I am going to be somewhere, so outside of Paris I seldom book ahead. See below, Where to Stay, pp. 54–56.

When to Go

Most people will go during the summer, but France's moderate climate allows for walking throughout the entire year. This does not mean that you will necessarily enjoy a walk along the Normandy coast in January, but, particularly in the south, many trails will be easily accessible throughout the entire year.

What to Bring

Money

With the less-than-impressive dollar hovering around 5.5 French francs, I budget about $75 (£50) per day if I am travelling alone. I find that an extra person adds about $35 (£22) to the expenses, adding up to about $110 (£72) per day. I usually carry about $400

(£260) worth of francs in cash, the rest in travellers checks also in francs. Travellers checks, in francs, are accepted at many hotels and some restaurants. However, since most proprietors seem to prefer cash or credit cards, I usually change travellers checks at a bank and pay cash for most transactions. Visa and Mastercard are almost universally accepted.

Luggage

I bring one backpack, which serves as check-in luggage. It carries almost everything except books, guides, maps, and other expensive items. You may wish to purchase a pack that has a disappearing suspension system as an alternative to a wilderness pack.

I use what will be my hiking daypack as carry-on luggage. I own a Lowe Klettersack, which is incredibly durable, comfortable, and capacious. My third piece is a small shoulder bag that contains photographic equipment, mini cassette recorder, and a few other small items. When I arrive at the airport or park my car, I put the large pack on my back, strap the camera bag around my neck, hold the daypack with both arms, and stagger to my destination. I avoid bringing more than I can carry in one trip.

Clothing

Including what I am wearing on the plane, I bring four shirts, three pairs of pants, one pair of shorts, two pairs of regular socks, three pairs of wool hiking socks, four pairs of underpants, one hat, one sweater, one lightweight jacket, one pair of hiking boots, and one pair of walking shoes. Everything is color coordinated and can be easily washed and dried. Although I become quickly tired of these clothes, they are sufficient for months of touring and can be easily burned upon return from France.

Personal/Health Items

Always bring soap, since some lodgings do not feel obligated to assure that their clients are sparkling clean. I also bring multiple vitamins, which I usually forget to take, razors, scissors, dental floss, toothbrush/paste, Ace Bandages for possible sprains, aspirin or aspirin substitute, bandaids, and toilet paper, which is not available at all French toilets. I do not bother with shampoo or conditioner, but you may have more hair and find bar-soap to be an inadequate hair cleanser. Female travellers may want to import tampons, which are inordinately expensive in France.

Miscellaneous

Sewing needles and thick thread are useful for torn clothes, lost buttons, and damaged equipment. I always bring a high-quality small flashlight that runs on AA batteries to fend off uninvited darkness. An extra, easily-compressed small backpack is convenient for shopping around town and carrying laundry. I also carry a small towel, which I have not yet employed for any task; however, I fear excluding it from my pack because I suspect that it will, at an unspecified future date, rescue me from some acute emergency situation. A small am-fm radio may break the silence of a televisionless hotel room. A lightweight electronic alarm will prod you from bed and ensure promptness to important transportation occurrences. I never go on any trip, foreign or domestic, without a lightweight goosedown sleeping bag. I have a North Face Light Rider, which weighs about two pounds and compresses to almost invisibility. A sleeping bag makes an excellent extra blanket and is indispensable when unrolled in its large storage sack as an extra large pillow that can allow you to sit comfortably upright on a bed with your head against the wall or headboard.

Daypack

On day hikes, I carry a Lowe Klettersac, which, as I have mentioned, is strong a durable. It has a top pocket and is also large enough to carry the numerous items listed below. The Klettersac also has a narrow waistbelt that distributes some of the weight from my shoulders to my hips. The waistbelt also prevents the pack from shifting at some critical juncture where I might be sent hurtling into an uninviting abyss. Even if you are not carrying much weight, be certain to purchase a pack with well-padded straps and a waistbelt.

I am not able to enjoy a simple walk without a vast catalogue of items that are designed to ward off any and every conceivable problem. I envy the occasional person I see strolling down a remote trail wearing a disintegrating pair of sandals and carrying nothing more than a leaking bottle of mineral water. I have never had the spiritual levity that allows these people to face possible disaster or even discomfort with such nonchalance.

The items you select from the following list for your daypack will depend upon where you fall on the nonchalance/paranoia continuum. I will discuss my rationale for carrying and frequency of use of each item.

The most important item in or on your daypack is water. I prefer the taste of water that is carried in clear, unbreakable lexan bottles with a loop top that prevents the tragedy of lost bottle caps. I use the one-liter size that can be inserted into nylon bottle-holders. The bottle-holders have a velcro loop that can be placed over belts, and I loop one around an adjustment strap on the side of my pack. Depending on the length of the walk, I also carry one or two extra bottles in the pack where they stay cooler. Do not pick up a bottle of mineral water, throw it in your pack, and assume that you have a safe supply of water. Once, having lost a canteen the day before, I placed a bottle of mineral water in my wife's pack. After climbing twenty-five minutes directly uphill in cloudless heat, we threw down our packs. The sound of breaking plastic and flowing water has never been so grim. About 40% of our water supply for that day soaked the contents of my wife's pack. I do not remember the exact outcome, but we probably barely survived while trading ill-natured and acrimonious accusations. Had we gotten lost, our bones could still be blanching somewhere in Europe. Use only indestructible water containers, and do not lose them.

Powdered water additives such as Gatorade can be purchased

in many larger supermarkets. They strike me as being expensive, but on longer, electrolyte-unbalancing walks I occasionally use them. They are also useful if you become weary of the taste of plain warm water.

On most walks, you will carry food. I usually bring some type of whole-grain bread, and I always have a supply of emergency *gauffrettes*. *Gauffrettes* are the chocolate or vanilla wafers that cause me to gain several pounds during a summer of walking. Most people have more sophisticated culinary desires and will be pleased with the variety of foods available even in smaller stores. For me, picnics involve too much organizing and general psychological stress. However, I realize that not everyone is going to find happiness sitting on a rock while gnawing on a loaf of bread. If you enjoy the eating aspect of walking, I refer you to the articles by Herb McGrew in *Gourmet* magazine (May 1989, Sept. 1990, May 1991, Aug. 1992). This pedestrian (in his form of locomotion, not choice of foods) gourmet and his *bon vivant* companions offer an affable connoisseur's guide to the Chemin St-Jaques and Provence.

I suspect that the concept of ozone depletion is actually a massive conspiracy by the world's sunscreen manufacturers; but, like an atheist who prays occasionally at bedtime, I am not sure and prepare for all possible outcomes. I do not like the slippery feel of sunscreen, and I still cannot bring myself to smear it on my balding, some say bald, head. However, I usually remember to put it on my face and arms. The best I have found is Coppertone's Sport SPF 30, which clings tenaciously to my skin rather than dripping into my eyes. However, if the price escalates from the present $17/£12 for four ounces, only the wealthiest of walkers will be able to afford its protection. Purchase sunscreen before you leave; in France it is even more expensive.

Although I seldom have blisters, I always include a package of Dr. Scholl's Moleskin in my daypack. Moleskin and similar products attach to skin in order to prevent sensitive spots from becoming blisters through frequent rubbing against a boot. I have used Moleskin on several occasions, and it has saved me from some painful miles. I also carry a small pair of scissors to properly shape the Moleskin.

As I mentioned before, toilet paper should always be kept within arms' reach. There are few toilets on trails and even fewer with toilet paper. Since toilets and reading material are frequently associated items, I should mention that I always bring a book, magazine, or newspaper on a walk. You may be trapped in a situation where you must wait for public transportation, or you may find an alluring spot that begs you to peruse that *Time* magazine whose covers you have been dying to get between.

I have lightweight binoculars that usually stay in my pack. Although they are seldom used, they can be valuable on less-frequently-marked trails that cross many treeless, rockless open fields. Binoculars enable you to scan distant rocks and trees for waymarks.

A mini-cassette recorder can be useful for recording thoughts and experiences while on the trail. I also use it to record trail sounds, such as singing birds, quick moving rivers, and occasional conversations.

Although I counsel that you should always pack a poncho or other rain protection, I frequently leave it behind on sunny days. Of course, weather can change quickly in France and, proving my inability to learn from experience, I have been deeply saturated on several poncholess walks. In cooler weather, I also bring a nylon jacket, which, however, I seldom use.

A map pouch that you can suspend from your body is also indispensable. Silva and other companies make a variety of these pouches which should be waterproof and fasten with velcro tabs. They keep your maps and guides visible but dry and also store a variety of other small items.

Trail Garb: Not GQ

I usually wear lightweight cotton pants and shirts. I seldom wear shorts, but then neither do Arabs in the burning desert. In addition to blocking harmful UV rays, pants offer protection from dense, thorny overgrown trails and the clinging insects they harbor. Although all of the trails in this book are in good condition, it is not uncommon for uncovered legs to suffer abrasive attacks on some segments.

Since jogging or walking shoes do not offer tender soles enough protection from the frequently rocky trails, hiking boots always adorn my valuable feet. Also, because of rain and intersecting streams, trails will be frequently muddy. If you wear walking or jogging shoes on a damp trail, they will become quickly inundated. I own two pairs of Vasque Sundowners, which currently retail for about $150 (£100). They are leather with a waterproof Gore-Tex lining and do not weigh heavily on my feet. They are the most comfortable boots that I have owned, but the soles seem to last only one summer. They can be resoled for about $50 (£35). If you do not currently own hiking boots, I suggest that you try several pairs before making a final decision.

I have both cotton and wool hiking socks. Both are comfortable, but I almost always wear the wool socks. I have no scientific explanation for this choice. I also have a hat which, unless it is raining, is found in my pack. A poncho and a nylon jacket, which I have already mentioned, complete my walking wardrobe.

2. When You Get There

I view France as being a rapidly changing nation, with the pace quickening in recent years. I believe that this nation can be divided into the tourist France, traditional France, and the France about to be: the suburbs where explosive growth is changing the nature of France.

The tourist France is not hard to identify. Anywhere a multitude of DROPS (see p. 3) are assembled is part of the tourist France. Normally DROPS are herded by bus between traffic-choked sites and will block your ability to enjoy a spiritual bonding with many otherwise wonderful sites. They also appear in most of your travel photos unless you arrive at your destination in the pre-dawn hours. Some DROPS who appear in my slides have had their faces permanently etched into my memory. In my mind, they are forever associated with France. I sometimes wonder who they are, where they are from, and why they are in my photos. I also wonder if I appear as a DROP in some stranger's photos.

Although France's great sights can be crowded with DROPS, particularly in July and August, they are not to be missed. If you are in Normandy or Brittany, you will want to visit Mont-St-Michel. In the Loire Valley, the popular *châteaux* such as Chenonceaux should be visited. Tourists come to these sorts of places because there is something to see. You should not shun them because other people will be sharing your experience. I have been to both Mont-St-Michel and Chenonceau during the peak of the tourist season in July. In both instances, the tour consisted of being swept by a wave of human motion through a memorable but turbulent monument. I have also visited both sites in early June when there were few tourists and sanity is more easily preserved.

If you can only visit popular monuments and areas during the peak period of July and August, brace yourself for a crowded, perhaps harrowing, experience. I seldom visit more than one tourist site per day, and I go with the attitude that I will be in and out quickly. For me, tourist sites usually serve as trail ends rather than goals.

The walks in this book will take you to and through many important tourist sites, but you should not limit yourself to this aspect of France. You will also want to visit what I call the traditional France, which most tourists see only through the window of a car, bus, or train. This is the walker's France, where the pace of life slows and few other tourists are seen. Here are rural towns and villages that adhere to rhythms and lifestyles that have been traditional in France for centuries. The towns may harbor a noteworthy Romanesque church, a small *château*, or nothing of any real historical significance. The walks described in this book will take you through many of these way-off-the-beaten-track towns, and you will frequently approach them on centuries-old footpaths. These are places that most travellers will bypass, but, having traversed them on foot, they will hold a special place in your memory.

The traditional France resides in vineyards, wheat fields, forests, hills, mountains, and even construction sites. It is also along streams, rivers, and sea coasts. You will pass through all of these on France's strikingly beautiful trails. You will see cows, goats, chickens, roosters, birds, butterflies, deer, rabbits, and many other denizens of the traditional landscape. You will hear water rushing, wind whizzing, birds chortling, and farm animals producing an assortment of cries, groans, and snorts. You will pass directly through the countrysides painted by Monet, Cézanne, Van Gogh, and many others. Twisted cityscapes of odd dimensions producing intense and peculiar shadows that should have been painted by De Chirico or Dali will also be scattered along your trails. As a walker, you will boldly go where few foreign tourists have gone before.

Tourist France and traditional France belong to the slow-to-die past. Tourist France will always exist, increasingly overrun by DROPS but always available for tourist yen. Traditional France is sinking slowly into obscurity. Many rural towns and villages have only ghosts and memories as inhabitants. Others shelter a few older people whose passing will mark the end of human habitation. Some villages will survive, but the population is now shifting from city and countryside to the France about-to-be, the suburbs.

Similar to the American move to the suburbs that began in the fifties and still continues, the French move to the suburbs is being fueled by the demand for reasonably-priced, single-family homes. In addition to homes, office buildings, shopping centers, hotels, restaurants, and entertainment complexes are being constructed in cinder block and corrugated steel at an expeditious pace and with little regard for aesthetics. Construction in the suburbs is creating jobs, which in turn creates more demand for housing. I do not know if this process will end, as in America, in exurbias and beyond, but suburbs are flourishing everywhere in France.

Presently, the suburbs are diminutive and do not extend far from the city center. Except in Paris and a few other large cities, the ride from the farthest suburban development to the center is usually no more than ten minutes. If a city has an expressway, the suburbs will develop along the exit(s). If there is no expressway, you will find it along one of the larger national routes.

For the traveller, the suburbs offer the opportunity for modern reasonably priced accommodations, inexpensive meals, easy parking, and abundant shopping. The suburbs are the clearest manifestation of contemporary France and its increasing emphasis on comfort and convenience. The stores, for example, are open at hours when people can shop, not the hours that are convenient for shopkeepers. Some people object to the suburban experience, claiming that it is senseless to travel to France in order to see suburbs and that somehow this is not the "real France." You will see few, if any, Americans or English in the suburbs, but you will see members of every French caste. You will ever see the overweight, tatooed French wearing stretch pants and muscle shirts that seem to have been banished from the more elegant cities and hidden from tourists.

Every trip to France should include time spent at tourist sites, the traditional countryside and cities, and the suburbs. Even if you do not think a visit to the suburbs is worthy of time spent in France, you should pass at least one night at a suburban hotel, eat at a chain restaurant such as Buffalo Grill, and shop at a mall. This experience will connect you with contemporary France and serve as strong contrast to an ordinary tourist vacation. Many of the walking tours in this book can easily be done from a suburban base (if you have a car) and will take you to notable tourist sites and through the traditional countryside.

Where to Stay

Because rooms are so abundant, I have listed few specific lodging suggestions. The easiest ways to find a room in France are to inquire at the local tourist office (*syndicat d'initiative* or *office de tourisme*), or simply walk around the town examining hotels, which always post their prices on the exterior of the building.

Having stayed in numerous quaint hotels, I now prefer to find more recently built accommodations with convenient parking. I find that many hotels with charming facades and lobbies are repositories for beds that were probably considered old in the seventeenth century. In larger areas, I also look for a hotel without a restaurant, which gives me more freedom to select where I wish to eat. I also avoid hotels that expect clients to eat breakfast.

If I cannot find a suitable recently built hotel in town with nearby free parking, I feel no regret in checking into a chain hotel in the suburbs. I prefer the one-star hotels that are becoming increasingly common throughout France. They usually cost between 155 and 180 francs for as many as three people, and usually offer a firm bed, private shower, toilet, and remote control color TV. My favorite chains include the Hotels Liberté, which feature large blue replicas of America's Statue of Liberty, Fast Hotels, which have a bellboy logo, and Bonsai Hotels, which have adopted a Japanese interior motif which they claim is more restful.

Two-star chain hotels tend to cost between 240 and 300 francs.

They have the same equipment but are more sturdily constructed, always have telephones, and frequently have a bathtub. They usually have a restaurant with undistinguished food, but there is no pressure to dine on site. The most common two-star hotel chains are the Hotels Campanile, Hotels Ibis, and Hotels Primavera.

Although I almost always stay at hotels, there are a variety of alternative accommodations available in France. If you go beyond the walks that I list in this book you may need to find one of the following types of accommodation. A *chambre d'hôte* is an accommodation in a private home. Breakfast is frequently included and dinner is often possible. Sometimes they have signs but often it is necessary to book through a tourist office. I have never been to a youth hostel, but in France they are usually dormitory-style accommodations called *auberges de jeunesse*. Seldom do they offer dinner, but they usually have kitchen facilities. *Gites d'étape* are similar to *auberges de jeunesse*, offering dormitory-style accommodations and kitchen privileges. They are established along trails, usually where no other lodging is available, and are frequently listed in the topo-guides. Camping opportunities are numerous and inexpensive in France, but the small size of individual sites requires much shoulder rubbing with your fellow campers. However, campgrounds are often attractively located and appear to be quieter than their American counterparts.

If you are accustomed to backpacking in North America, you will note that France has very little true wilderness, and non-designated camping along most of the trails in this book is forbidden. Non-designated camping is forbidden along public roads, the shores of the sea, within 200 meters of drinking water, on sites classified as protected, within 500 meters of historic monuments, and in areas forbidden by municipalities. On agricultural land and private forests, you are obligated to ask the permission of the owner. In spite of this list of forbidden areas, I have never seen government agents aggressively seeking illegally situated campers. Gypsies seem to camp anywhere and everywhere in France with a minimum of harassment, and a backpacker with proper equipment can probably find a suitable bivouac most nights. Along some trails, I have seen splendid sites suitable for camping while on other trails there appear to be few, if any, suitable camping opportunities.

Public Transportation: Trains, Buses, Taxis, Thumbs

Trains

If you are travelling through France by train, I refer you to the guidebooks I have mentioned above for general information. On a general train trip through France you will probably see only larger train stations, which will normally have a human (although not always humane) staff to assist you. The walks in this book will take you to some of the more remote stations where the ticket purchasing procedure has been automated. The ticket purchasing machine (*billeterie automatique*, also found in many stations that have a live staff) is usually found along the tracks by the now deserted train station. The machine is not difficult to operate, but you must have coins and correct change is usually necessary. Before entering the train, be certain to validate your ticket by punching it in an orange machine. Failure to do so can result in a stern lecture or stiff fine from the unhappy conductor.

Buses

Although there are some long-distance buses in France, they are primarily used for shorter regional transportation. The state rail system SNCF operates many buses in areas where, due to declining patronage, train service has been discontinued. Numerous private companies and individuals also service selected routes. Both are inexpensive and reliable. Schedules for SNCF buses and private lines can often be found at the train station or local tourist office. Necessary information for bus connections can be found in the trail notes for individual walks.

Taxis

Areas of France that are not served by public transportation can usually be reached by taxi. Many small towns and most medium-size towns will have at least one taxi. The taxi drivers will frequently perform multiple transportation roles by also serving as ambulance drivers and furniture movers, so they may not be available when you need a ride. If you require a taxi, reserve ahead. On certain walks, I have suggested the use of a taxi. This mode of transportation can be expensive for one person, but the cost per person can be quite reasonable if two or more people ride together. If there is a tourist office, they will help you locate a taxi. Otherwise consult your general guide book or inquire at a local café or hotel.

Hitchhiking

The use of a combination of car and public transportation or just public transportation is sufficient to complete all of the walks in this book. Nevertheless, I suspect that public transportation could often be replaced by what the French call *"autostop."* However, if you are in a hurry, plan ahead and use public transportation. Many of the roads along our trails are not frequently used and traffic is very local in nature.

Driving

Pros and Cons

Even though escape from cars and traffic is one of the goals of a walking vacation, there is no inconsistency in writing about driving in a walking book. Ironically, your car will enable you to more efficiently avoid other cars and also give you the freedom to set your own schedule. You will be free from strike-prone public transportation and able to reach places that are not served by public transportation. Although there are some negatives, including expense, heavy traffic, difficult parking in large cities, and poorly marked roads, I would not enjoy France as much without the freedom a car allows.

Finding Your Way

Due to poorly marked road signs, I usually spend more time lost on major French roads that I spend lost on remote trails. Unlike American or British road signs, which usually have the route number clearly indicated, the route number on French road signs is usually omitted. Most road signs are marked only with the name of a town, and the selection of which town names appear on signs strikes me as being capricious. Sometimes it will be a major city several hundred kilometers in the distance, while at other times it might be a hamlet a few kilometers down the road. This is fine for the locals who already know where they are, but tourists who do not know the name of every town along their route will be forced to make frequent map-consultation stops. Of course, just when you need to look at your map there will be no place to pull over, and a long line of DROP-driven vehicles will be pursuing you at a rapid clip. Avoid this problem by planning your route in advance.

Route Selection, Distance, Time

On a recent vacation, I foolishly drove 460 miles from Cahors in central France to Le Havre in Normandy. After $11 \frac{1}{2}$ hours of driving, I arrived delirious, almost unable to see, speak, or walk. Most of this hazardous, pollution-choked ride was completed on the *routes nationales* (national roads), which are usually two-lane roads marked red on most maps. These routes go directly between larger towns and, where there is no alternate autoroute (limited-access expressway) to divert traffic, they are clogged with some of the world's worst-polluting and slowest-moving trucks. You will often follow these dreadful vehicles in parade-like formation for miles on end with dozens of other tormented motorists. Avoid the *routes nationales*; you will usually average no better than 40 miles per hour even with the most limited stopping time.

If you are in a hurry, cruise along at eighty miles per hour on the multi-laned autoroutes. They are expensive but there is no other alternative if you are on a tight time schedule. Otherwise plan ahead and take the departmental routes, which are marked in yellow or white on most maps. Travel on these roads is slightly slower than on *routes nationales* due to the frequency of small towns, but there are few trucks or other cars. It is along these routes that you will develop fond memories of the French driving experience.

Purchasing Gas

When you receive your car, ask what type of gas it consumes. In France, there are three major types: *super* (which is regular leaded), *super sans plombe* (which is regular unleaded), and diesel. My most recent car took unleaded, which is becoming more common. Both *super* and *super sans plombe* cost about $4.00 (£2.75) per gallon. Diesel fuel is about $3.00 (£2.00) per gallon. Almost all gas stations are self service (*libre service*), and I have never been to a service station that required pre-payment.

Parking

Parking in most medium and large cities is *"payant."* If you do not see a meter, look for a sinister device known as the *"horodateur"* (hour dater). Emblazoned with a large "P," this machine devours coins and spits out a piece of paper that indicates the amount of time you can legally park your car. Place it in your car so that it is visible from the driver's side window.

At some parking lots, you do not pay as you exit with your car. You must pay at a machine in or near the parking lot. When you locate the machine, insert the ticket that you received upon entry. The machine will indicate how much you must pay. Insert your coins and retrieve your ticket, which you will place in another machine by the exit gate.

Dangers

France has the highest per capita traffic fatality rate in Western Europe. I believe that the fundamental cause for this frightening record is the high volume of slow-moving vehicles that litter most roads and the subsequent recklessness of impatient speeders. Trucks, buses, farm machinery, and people in cars that feel no need to arrive anywhere at any particular time force others to continuously pass them on narrow winding roads. Rendered insane by the slow pace and excessive pollution, I have too often taken what is called a "calculated risk." This is actually a foolish risk. Take no chances.

In the mountains, if you hear a horn honking directly in front of you, it means that a large object, bus or truck, is coming around a corner directly into your path. Slow down and surrender as much road as possible without scraping a mountain or tumbling over the side of a cliff. (Motion sickness pills can be especially useful for passengers during long, tortuous mountain rides.) If you are in the fast lane of a multi-laned highway, and the drivers of a vehicle directly behind you activates his left-turn signal, do not assume that he is indicating his intention to commit suicide by driving into oncoming traffic. This is a polite method of requesting that you move your car into a slower lane before he drives directly over you.

I have never had an accident in France, but I will briefly summarize what the French government considers to be your responsibilities. In the case of any accident, you must stop immediately. If the accident has only caused vehicular damage, you must exchange names and addresses with any other persons involved. If there has been bodily injury, and you are able, you must either render first aid or immediately seek emergency assistance from police, an ambulance service, or a doctor. Even if you are not involved, you are obliged to offer necessary aid until emergency vehicles arrive. Failure to comply with these rules can result in a two-month to two-year jail sentence and/or a 2,000 to 30,000 franc fine.

Only once in France has my unoccupied car been assaulted. I was hiking in the vicinity of highly-touristed Saint-Tropez and had parked my car on a road leading to the beach. When I returned, the driver's side door had a large dent, which was the result of an attempt by some as-of-yet-unapprehended individual to pull the door panel away from the glass of the driver's window. This would have allowed him to reach down and open the door. Luckily, he fled the scene before the completion of this heinous act. Do not leave anything of value in your car or keep items such as maps or tour guides that identify you as a tourist visible to passers-by. If your car is burglarized, you must go to the local *gendarmerie* (police station) and file a report for insurance purposes.

Men at Work

During the summer months, France's roads are constantly being repaired. Some roads are simply blocked with no suggested detour, while others may have a couple of signs that take you from the construction site to nowhere in particular. Having been dropped unwillingly into the Kafkaesque nightmare of only being able to approach, but not attain, your destination, you will often feel unjustly persecuted. You must be prepared. Be certain to have a detailed road map. I always drive with the Michelin road atlas on the passenger seat or on a passenger's lap.

Militant Road Closers

Any group that uses vehicles to complete a task usually feels free to blockade roads in order to protest supposed slights and grievances. The French agricultural community occasionally displays a rather un-Green-Acre-like militancy, which manifests itself in bizarre convoys of farm equipment worthy of a Mad Max film. These convoys can easily close roads and entire cities. Fortunately, the farmers get hungry around dinnertime and go home. More nomadic truck drivers can block roads for days and even weeks. During the summer of 1992, they paralyzed traffic throughout the entire nation for more than ten days. Many people found them-selves trapped in cars or tourist buses for days on end. Even psy-chopathic taxi drivers, in a reprise of Robert De Niro's famous role, sometimes find satisfaction in holding their urban neighbors hostage in narrow, crowded city streets.

Protect yourself by watching the news and glancing at newspa-per headlines. Even if you do not understand French, the aerial photos of highway chaos will alert you to the possibility of road closings. Under such circumstances, plan your route carefully along the minor departmental roads, which are usually forgotten by the militants. During the height of the truck-drivers' blockade in 1992, when virtually every autoroute and *route nationale* was impassa-ble, I heroically drove the eighty miles from Amiens to the Aeroport Roissy-Charles de Gaulle in about $2\,^1/_2$ hours down a series of about fifteen departmental routes. Under normal conditions, us-ing the autoroute, this same trip would have taken just over an hour. However, under these extraordinary circumstances, I was fortunate to reach the airport at all. People who took the auto-route are probably still sleeping in their cars.

Communication

If you are going to use telephones in France, purchase a *télécarte*, which, unless you are calling an emergency number or the operator, you must insert into almost any pay phone in order to complete a call. The least expensive is forty francs. It can be purchased at post offices, railroad stations, and many *tabacs* (tobacco stands). Although on a nationwide basis most phones are operated with a *télécarte*, your walks will take you to more remote areas where you will frequently encounter coin-operated phones. I have found that most of these no longer function, but if you find one in working condi-tion, insert at least one franc, wait for the dial tone, then dial.

If you wish to mail a letter or post card from France, go to the local PTT (post office), where you can purchase envelopes and stamps. For a short letter, you should pay less than five francs for an envelope and a stamp. Literary giants and those unable to omit any exciting detail about their trip should ask the clerk to weigh the letter and affix the proper postage.

Laundromats

In many larger towns, and in all cities, you will be able to do your laundry in a laundromat. In France, these are usually called *"lavomatique"* or *"lavabo."* The tourist office or your hotel staff will be able to direct you to one. Although they are not always alike in detail, the basic procedure is the same as in the U.S. and Britain— wash clothes, dry clothes. However, this is usually easier said than done. Some machines taken certain combinations of coins, while others require what is called a *"jeton,"* which you purchase either from a machine on the wall or from the proprietor. The combination of coins is never the same, and even though I hoard coins, I never seem to have the correct combination. Sometimes you can get change at the laundromat, but when you most need it none will be available. Do not count on the other patrons for change. You will see most of them standing around scratching their heads and shaking coins with the same blank look that occupies your own face. Find a nearby store and make a small purchase, or, with tears in your eyes, you may even try to ask for change from hardened clerks who have no interest in helping someone else's customers.

Coins in hand, your tribulations are not over. You will also need detergent. Usually the laundromat has a machine that dispenses detergent. Again, you need coins or a *jeton*. The detergent will come either as a small packet or fall directly from a machine. If it falls directly from a machine be certain to use one of the cups lying around the laundromat to catch it; otherwise your detergent will have to be scraped from the floor before being introduced into the washing machine. If you are travelling by car, it is best to purchase detergent at a grocery store. Not only is it cheaper, but the soap machine at the *lavomatique* may be *"en panne"* or *"hors service"* (out of order).

The soap usually goes into a slot on top of the machine where it says *"lavage,"* and normally you press a single button in order to start the machine. Frequently this button is red; if you do not see a red button ask for help or take your chances. Good luck! Drying is a similar but less complicated procedure. The dryer will usually accept two- or five-franc coins or a *jeton*.

French laundromats are not cheap. Recently, at St-Malo, I spent 38 francs ($7/£4.50) for a single load: 20 francs for washing, 2 francs for detergent, and 16 francs for drying. However, the alternative, walking around in perpetually dirty clothes, is no fun and is certain to arouse scorn and suspicion in those you encounter.

3. Trail Life

Waymarking

All trails in this book are waymarked, meaning you will be able to find your way by looking for painted marks on trees, rocks, fence posts, utility poles, etc. In France, a waymark is called a *flèche* (arrow) and a waymarked trail is *balisée*. Almost all of the trails in this book have been waymarked with one red bar directly over one white bar. If you see a such a waymark, you should continue straight. A change of direction is indicated by a double waymark, meaning that you will see four alternating red and white bars. Sometimes there will be an arrow indicating the exact change of direction, while at other times you must search for the correct turn. You will also see standard red and white waymarks painted over with a single diagonal bar. This is a diverticulum waymark, which usually leads from the trail into an urban area and vice versa.

In many areas, there will be more than one set of waymarks, so it is important to remember that a single white waymark or a single red waymark is not equivalent to a red and a white waymark. Someone did not forget to paint the second bar; the single waymarks you see are for different trails. Always look for the red and white waymarks unless the trail notes specify otherwise.

The waymarks are designed to help you overcome the ever-present terror of being lost and unable to ask for directions. They are your security blanket; do not lose sight of them. In general, you should never walk more than five minutes beyond a junction where a change of direction is possible without seeing a waymark. If you do not see a waymark within a short period of time, return to the last waymark and search carefully for the correct direction. If you have not found a waymark in forty-five minutes you will probably never be seen again.

On some trails, there are few trees, rocks, utility poles, or fence posts to mark. On such trails, usually over open fields, you may go long periods without seeing a waymark. You must read this book's trail notes carefully, and be vigilant in watching for change-direction waymarks. These may appear some distance before the actual turn. Overreacting to such waymarks, I have plunged wildly into virtually impassible bush and stumbled insanely down precipitous drops. Search for a logical place to turn, which will almost always be a clearly marked trail.

In spite of the volunteers' efforts to clearly waymark trails, you can run into problems. In some cases, trails have been incompetently marked. In other cases, waymarks have, with age, faded to almost invisibility or have been painted over by zealous utility-post painters. I have noted these problems in the trail notes and provided suggestions that should prevent you from becoming lost.

Having returned home after a summer of walking in France, you will be looking everywhere, even in your own house, for the guidance and security of the red and white waymarks.

Use of Topo-Guides, Maps, and Trail Notes

An excellent sense of direction is not needed to complete any of the walks in this book. I often become lost in small buildings and can never find my car in a parking lot. You may, however, wish to learn the fundamentals of map and compass use.

Topo-guides (see pp. 40–42) are illustrated with 1:50,000 maps of the trails that you will use. This is a large enough scale for any of the walks suggested in this book. The trail is marked in red and is usually quite accurately depicted. However, it is important to remember that the trail can change as a result of road building, changing agricultural activity, loss of the right of passage, etc. This means that your map may not indicate the exact course of the current trail. It may happen that the map indicates a certain direction that conflicts with the direction that the waymarks indicate. In such cases, always follow the waymarks.

The maps in the topo-guides, and the supplemental maps that I suggest you purchase, are topographical. Topographical maps use what are called "contour lines" to give a detailed picture of how the land is shaped. If you know how to read a topographical map, you will be able to visualize where, how often, and how steeply you must climb on each walk. You will also be able to locate natural features such as lakes and rivers and man-made objects such as buildings and utility wires.

You should also purchase a compass with a transparent, rectangular base plate that can be used in conjunction with a topograhical map. They are inexpensive and can always indicate in what direction you are travelling. If you follow the trail notes in this book, you will probably not need a compass. However, if you experiment with other trails or absent-mindedly wander off the trails described in this book, there is always the possibility of becoming lost. Knowing how to use a map and compass has helped me stay found on a number of occasions. *Staying Found* by June Fleming (New York: Vintage, 1982) is clearly written and will teach you more than you ever wished to know about staying found.

If you do not learn from books, try orienteering. This is a rapidly growing international competitive sport. You are given a map and are required to find your way as quickly as possible through varied terrain. Along the way you must record certain codes that will prove that you have touched all points on a required route. There are several levels of competition, and novices are welcome. For more information, contact the United States Orienteering Federation, P.O. Box 1444, Forest Park, GA 30051.

The trail notes that describe the thirty-five trails included in the final section of this book are designed to be used with the map we have provided; they can also be used in conjunction with the topo-guide or topographical map that I have suggested you purchase for each walk. The primary purpose of the trail notes is to alert you to problems that may be encountered along the trail. These problems usually consist of ambiguous waymarks or no waymarks at all.

The trail notes appear in sequential order, meaning that the problem described in trail note two comes directly after the problem described in trail note one. Since it is very difficult to accurately describe most map locations, I usually provide a physical description of the problem area and sometimes make a notation as to how many hours and minutes into the walk the problem occurs. Of course everyone walks at a different pace, but this should not present a serious problem. For example, if you arrived at the problem spot given in the sample trail note above in thirty minutes, you would know that you are walking slightly faster than my pace. If you continue at this pace, you will encounter the problems described sooner than I have noted.

On level terrain, I tend to walk about 3–3 $^1/_3$ miles per hour, whereas on hilly or more rugged terrain I walk at about 2 $^1/_2$–2 $^2/_3$ miles per hour. All of the times given are actual walking times. Periods of rest are not included. Wear a watch that also functions as a stopwatch, and remember to turn it off while you are not walking.

You should review the trail notes before departure and anticipate the problems described as you are walking. If I do not make any comments, it means that at the time of writing there were no problems, and the trail was clearly marked. I have attempted to carefully present an accurate description of the problems encountered in the trail notes and accompanying maps. I believe that I have succeeded, but if what you see on the trail contradicts what I have written, let your eyes be your guide. As I have mentioned, the trail and its markings can change—so be flexible. Unless you are very experienced with a map and compass or have much time at your disposal for being lost, you should stay on the waymarked trail. Sometimes I see a tempting shortcut or an interesting feature on the map that would take me off the trail only to rejoin it again at some distant point. Sometimes I am lucky, while at other times I become lost (but not hopelessly lost). Common sense should keep you from making any serious errors.

How Often/How Far

I have included walks that are anywhere from two to nine miles, with most in the four-to-six-mile range. Even if you only embark on an occasional short walk, you will experience France as have few other foreign tourists.

Do not become obsessed with distance. This is not a competitive sport, and there is no point in consuming entire days with walking. You are on vacation and should enjoy not only the walks but the destinations. A four-to-six-mile walk will take you into the countryside and onto local public transportation for several hours. You will also get enough exercise to justify a calorie-laden dinner and will be tired enough to sleep well at night. Also remember that you will often be walking several miles around tourist sites and your home base during the evening. A day in which you complete a six-mile walk can easily add up to a ten-mile walking day with such incidental walking.

Time of Day

In less travelled areas, you will occasionally have to arrange your walking schedule around available transportation. However, many areas have excellent public transportation and you can often arrange the walks to fit your general schedule.

When I have a choice, I usually stagger onto the trail at about ten or eleven a.m. This is in contrast to conventional wisdom, which counsels early rising in order to beat the midday heat. Since I am never in any hurry to rise early and rush to any destination, I spend many days walking in the noon-day sun with only the occasional mad dog or Englishman as a companion.

Potential Problems

France's trails are almost always havens of tranquility with nothing to fear. I have never felt threatened by humans I have encountered, but other problems can arise that you should be aware of. Although none of the following problems are life threatening, they can be disagreeable.

Dog Days: Lots of Bark

Rural France is dog country, and many unemployed dogs have little else to do beyond sunning themselves and barking at the occasional pedestrian. Fortunately, almost all dogs are chained or confined to their yard by steel fences. You might occasionally, however, encounter loose dogs (although on the thirty-five trails mentioned in this book, I cannot think of a single loose-dog encounter).

Here are the tips provided by the Michigan Humane Society for individuals confronted by dogs:

* Do not run. Stand still and remain calm.
* Do not look at the dogs. Direct eye contact may be taken as a threat.
* Do not yell or throw things at the dogs. Screams or quick gestures will scare them and may cause an attack.
* Do not approach a dog pack. Walk away facing them so as not to expose your back to them.
* If attacked, curl up to cover your neck, head, and chest with your arms and legs. Do not struggle or fight back; play dead.
* If bitten, stay calm and when safe, leave the area and wash the wound with warm water and contact a doctor or emergency room.

I have never encountered the type of dog that is trained to attack or for that matter trained to do anything at all. There are no rabid bands of pit bull terriers ready to tear unwary walkers to pieces. However, in any encounter with a dog you should not show fear. Make it obvious that you are the master of the situation and the dog risks having its fangs knocked down its throat if it approaches you.

Bugsy

The first year I walked in France, I brought a net to wear over my head and face. I was accustomed to walking in the mosquito and black fly infested North Woods, where the unprotected human can emerge with a bitten and all but unrecognizable face and body. In France it is not necessary to take any unusual precautions against bugs and, in subsequent years, the net has remained at home. I have not missed it. In fact, I have encountered more mosquitoes in unscreened hotel rooms than I have on trails. Although no general bug problem exists, on heavily-wooded portions of some trails there are numerous non-biting bugs. If you are on such a trail do not breathe deeply unless you enjoy inhaling foreign objects. If you do inhale a bug it will be unpleasant but probably not dangerous.

Spiders themselves are not a problem, but their webs can be tiresome. Occasionally, while on narrow, damp forest trails, your face will have frequent close encounters with spider webs. Normally, you will not be able to see them until they are wrapped around your face. In such areas, I suggest that you carry a walking stick before you in order to break the webs before they must be scraped from your insulted countenance. I have never yet been caught in a web that I could not escape from.

Bees are not a problem, and I seldom notice any while I am walking. However, fields of wild flowers will often grace your path, and where there are flowers, there are bees. You will probably never be menaced by a bee, but if you are allergic to bee stings, you should bring the proper medication and always walk with a companion.

Heaven's Gate: The Grass Is Always Greener

Sometimes in rural areas you will have to cross fields that require you to open and close a gate. The gates are not there to keep you out, they are designed to keep grazing animals from seeking the greener grass on the other side. Occasionally, the gate is hinged and simply latched with some familiar looking device. Usually, however, it is a non-hinged, barbed-wire gate that is held by wire to a fence post. To open such a gate, push the gate post towards the fence post and pull the wire over the gate post, which will release the gate. Sometimes this takes considerable strength. Once through, close the gate and replace the wire. You may also see steps that allow you to climb fences and will probably continue to see them until cows learn to climb steps.

None of the thirty-five trails in this book require you to walk through fields of livestock. However, if you plan to do other walking in France, adhere to the following advice. Before entering such areas, it is wise to check cattle underbodies in an attempt to ascertain sex. Udders are a good sign; anything else can present a problem. Only once did I have a bull session. While crossing a pasture on a remote rural trail, I noticed a large, horned object gaining on me. Between me and the horned object were several udder-bearing beasts. I was not sure whether the horny bull was pursuing the cows or me. However, not considering myself to be a suitable mate, I ran to the nearest exit, not bothering to look back. If you notice a bull in a field that you must cross, make a clear mental note as to where you are supposed to exit the field. Then, if possible, follow the fence around to your destination so that in case of emergency you can slip under the fence and into safety. Otherwise, take the farthest possible course around the bull, watching carefully for possible emergency exits.

Road Warrior

Sometimes you will be forced to walk along roads with frequent traffic. Fortunately this does not happen too often. If you are walking down such a road, be aware that unbridled French traffic travels at no snail's pace, and the road shoulders are often minimal. These factors, combined with the tortuous nature of many roads, can make even a short walk an intense experience. Walk on the side of the road that has the widest shoulder or, shoulders being equal, the side where drivers can best see you. This is not always in the direction of oncoming traffic. If a car is coming, it is safest to stop walking, back away as far as possible from the road, and watch carefully. After one car has passed, look carefully to see if another is following closely behind; its sound may be disguised by the sound of the first car.

The Car: Where to Leave It

I prefer to leave the car at my final destination and take the bus or train back to my walk's starting point. This procedure assures me that my car, barring theft, will be there to transport me to my hotel when I have completed a walk. Also, I agonize over problems that might arise with public transportation: a misread or obsolete schedule, a strike, acts of a supreme deity, etc. If you do not cherish the thought of being marooned at walk's end, leave your car at your destination.

Part Two

35 Great Walks

How to Use the
Thirty-Five Walk Descriptions

Each walk listed below is organized into the following information:

1. **Key to Symbols:** One or more of the following symbols will be found in the box at the beginning of each walk description to give you an idea of what to expect to see on the way:

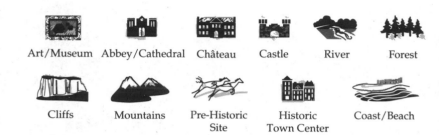

Art/Museum   Abbey/Cathedral   Château   Castle   River   Forest

Cliffs   Mountains   Pre-Historic Site   Historic Town Center   Coast/Beach

2. The **General Description**, which is a short compendium of the topography and historical sites that you will encounter along the route. No attempt has been made to be comprehensive, and it is suggested that you consult the guidebooks mentioned above and other sources for more comprehensive historical information.

3. The **Optional Maps/Topo-Guides** section provides you with specific information about maps and topo-guides (see pp. 40–42) that may make your walking experience more interesting, especially if you enjoy working with a topographical map or desire to expand your walking adventures in a particular area. The Série Bleu maps are marked with a number and a letter for easy identification and the topo-guides are marked by their trail route number, a reference number, and the name of the trail. All of this information is provided in this section.

4. The **Time/Distance** section includes the length of time necessary to complete the walk at a rate of about 2 $^1/_2$–3 miles per hour and the distance in miles and kilometers.

5. The location of **Toilet Facilities** along the trail has been included. Often, however, there are none, which is why information has also been included on the amount of privacy. In general, men should have little trouble relieving themselves anywhere along the trail. On trails where much privacy has been indicated, women should also have no problems. Even where a trail is noted as having little privacy, women will usually have a number of suitable opportunities. Also, remember that you can usually use toilets at cafés, restaurants, and train stations.

6. Where you can obtain **Refreshments**, either at a restaurant or café, has also been noted. However, do not neglect to bring water with you on any walk.

7. Instructions on how to arrive at the starting point via automobile and public transportation have been included in the **Getting There** section.

8. The **Trail Notes** correspond to the map, and indicate the general course of the trail. They have been structured so that they may be marked with a check after corresponding landmarks have been achieved. Although the inclusion of a note does not necessarily indicate a problem, notes have been provided wherever problems exist. In any case, always watch for waymarks and study your map.

9. At the end of each section, some **Suggestions for More Walking** have been included. Wherever possible, other day walks have been included, as well as possibilities for shortening or extending each of the thirty-five selected walks.

Walk 1: Monet's Water Lilies: Giverny

Walk: **Vernon to Giverny**

General Description

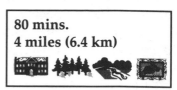

80 mins.
4 miles (6.4 km)

This wonderful walk between two outstanding sites begins at Vernon, an attractive riverside town where Monet began painting churches. Fourteenth-century Eglise Notre-Dame, rendered ethereal by Monet's atmospheric paintings, merits a visit, as does the remains of the eleventh-century *château*, which was constructed by the English King Henry I. Wandering about the town, where you may lodge and dine comfortably in close proximity to master Monet's florid heritage, note the lovely homes, some dating back to the fifteenth century.

Departing Vernon on a bridge over the Seine River, watch for the beautiful cliffs that form a dramatic backdrop for your trek along a rails-to-trails path that offers the nostalgic joy of partially-exposed railway ties; enjoy excellent views of the Seine and Vernon as you whistle-stop your way to the water lilies. Soon you will climb into an emerald green forest known intimately by Monet and essentially unchanged by encroaching civilization. Emerging from forested tranquility, you will descend quickly into Giverny along secluded rural tracks.

Monet, himself trekking along this alluring segment of the Seine River, decided to rent the property that now forms Le Musée Claude Monet. Here, where he spent more than forty years and where he died in 1926, Monet painted his most famous series, the *Water Lilies*. Follow the footsteps of the great Impressionist master as you stroll about the garden that houses the renowned Japanese-style bridge and the world-class water lilies. Visit Claude's residence/studio and wander about the little hamlet that was home to one of the finest modern painters.

Optional Maps/topo-guides: Série Bleu 2113 ouest; GR 2 (ref. #203) Les Falaises de la Seine: Triel-sur-Seine—Le Havre

---

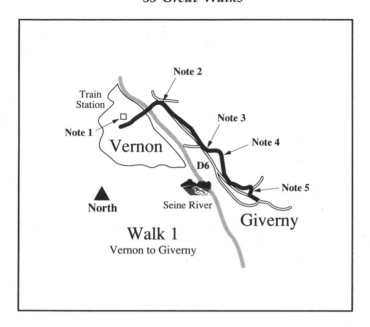

Time/Distance: 1 hour 20 minutes/4 miles (6.4 kilometers)

Difficulties: A strenuous ten-minute climb about midway

Toilet Facilities: None, but some privacy

Refreshments: Vernon, Giverny

Getting There: From the parking lot at Giverny, directly across from the Monet museum, three buses per day make the quick trip to Vernon's train station. Schedules are posted at Giverny or at Vernon's train station. (Trains to Vernon run from Paris or Rouen every 2–3 hours.) If bus schedules do not fit your schedule, it would not be too difficult to walk both ways.

Trail Notes

___ 1a. From the train station, which is at place de la Gare, turn left (your back is to the station) down a narrow road called rue Emile Steiner.

___ 1b. At the first cross street, rue Ambroise Bully, turn right.

___ 1c. A couple of minutes later, at the traffic circle, turn left onto the main street, rue d'Albufera, and follow it to the bridge over the Seine.

___ 2. As you cross the bridge over the Seine, make the first possible right where you see a red and white waymark on a metal utility pole.

___ 3. Watch to your left for a waymark that leads you from the railway bed and onto a narrow, wooded trail.

___ 4. About midway into the walk, while walking through the forest, you will see a waymark indicating a right turn. DO NOT turn right until you reach a clearing where you will turn right onto a wide path which is marked.

___ 5. You will approach Giverny from the heights and be able to see this cluster of buildings. When you reach an asphalt road just above the town you will see an "X" straight ahead. Turn right here and descend into Giverny.

Suggestions for More Walking

It is possible to extend this walk to 12 miles by leaving your car at Bonniers-sur-Seine and taking the train to Vernon and then walking back via the GR 2 trail (GR = *grande randonnée*) and a marked diverticulum. The diverticulum is only partially indicated in the above mentioned topo-guide, so you should have the Série Bleu map 2113 ouest. Another excellent and short walk will take you about four miles between Bouafles and historic Andelys (about 20 miles northwest on D313 from Vernon) passing by the magnificent ruins of Château Gaillard. Buses pass between the two towns (tel. gare routière des Andelys 32 39 40 60).

Walk 2: Rouen

Walk: La Fontaine to Saint-Martin-de-Boscherville

General Description

| 90 mins. |
| 4.5 miles (7.2 km) |

Rouen, in spite of its infamy as the final burning place of Joan of Arc, is one of the most attractive and accommodating of today's large French cities. A walking tour of the Rive Droite (the right bank, north of the Seine) will take you along narrow passages lined with impeccably-restored, timber-framed homes dating back as far as the fifteenth century. Walk along rue St-Romain and then rue Rollon to the place du Vieux-Marche, where Joan met her demise. Punctuating the rows of fine homes are several Gothic masterpieces, including the Cathedrale de Notre Dame that Monet painted endlessly. Museums also abound—the not-to-be-missed Musée des Beaux Arts, for example, houses a superb collection of Impressionist and post-Impressionist paintings.

In spite of its size, Rouen is close to unspoiled rural tranquility; a quick bus ride will take you from big city to rustic obscurity where today's walk begins.

Ascending from diminutive, riverside La Fontaine you will be greeted by expansive views of the Seine River valley. Soon the views become partially occluded as you walk high among dense stands of forest. Descending from the forest, the abbey appears majestically medieval as you begin to approach Saint-Martin from lofty cliffs lining the lovely Seine. The eleventh-century Abbaye St-Georges is a remote masterpiece of Romanesque architecture encompassed in a comely, arcadian assemblage of ancient homes and scarcely-frequented cafés and stores. This is a good place to linger before returning to the twentieth century.

Optional Maps/topo-guides: Série Bleu 1911 ouest; GR 2 (ref. #203) Les Falaises de la Seine: Triel-sur-Seine—Le Havre

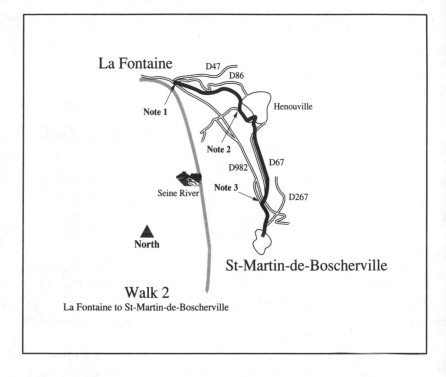

La Fontaine

D47

D86

Note 1

Henouville

Note 2

D982

D67

Seine River

Note 3

D267

North

St-Martin-de-Boscherville

Walk 2

La Fontaine to St-Martin-de-Boscherville

Time/Distance: 1 hour 30 minutes/4.5 miles (7.2 kilometers)

Difficulties: A five-minute climb out of La Fontaine

Toilet Facilities: None, but much privacy

Refreshments: Saint-Martin-de-Boscherville

Getting There: SATAR buses 30a and 30b run frequently along D982 from Rouen to Le Havre, connecting both towns on today's walk and a variety of other interesting small towns. Schedules are available at the tourist office or *gare routière* (bus station) (tel. 35 71 23 29) at Rouen. They are also posted at all bus stops along the way. Take the bus from Saint-Martin-de-Boscherville (the bus stops along D982 and does not go into the city center or to the abbey) to La Fontaine.

Trail Notes

__ 1a. From the covered bus stop walk west in the direction that the bus continues for a couple of minutes, looking to the right.

__ 1b. Make the first possible right turn onto D86, where you will see a sign "Henouville 3 km." (Do not continue west along D65 where you will also see red and white waymarks—be certain to turn right on D86.)

__ 1c. Once on D86 the road forks almost immediately: look to the right, and you will see a staircase that is waymarked and leads you to the trail. (The trail is well marked from this point to beyond Henouville, but watch carefully for waymarks in the forest.)

__ 2. After a long descent from Henouville, you will turn left onto a narrow asphalt road that you will follow for a while. The turn is well marked.

__ 3. When you reach D982 on your final approach to Saint-Martin, turn left and follow the road back to town.

Suggestions for More Walking

This walk can be easily extended an extra four miles by taking the same bus to Duclair: an attractively situated, bustling port town on the Seine with much commerce and an interesting church constructed between the twelfth and sixteenth centuries. Also, just west of Rouen and across the Seine lies the immense and beautiful Forêt de Roumare, which is easily accessible and provides miles of trails for exploration.

Walk 3: Normandy: Atlantic Cliff Walking

Walk: **Vattetot-sur-Mer to Etretat**

General description

**105 mins.
5 miles (8 km)**

A short, but unforgettable, excursion from Rouen (50 miles) or Honfleur (40 miles) to the Atlantic coast of Normandy will bring you to the famous cliffs of Etretat. The cliffs—painted by numerous artists, including Monet, Courbet, and Boudin—soar over two hundred feet and provide some of the most spectacular walking scenery available anywhere. If you have an extra day or two, enjoy sandy beaches, and wish to breathe clean ocean air, plan to spend some time in Etretat. Formerly a fishing village, now a resort, Etretat offers numerous accommodations, which the tourist office can help you book.

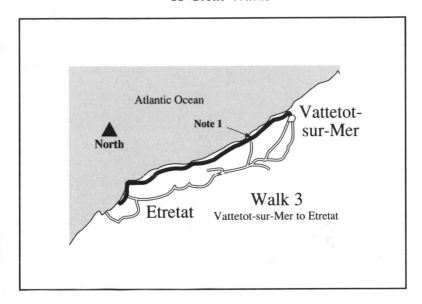

You will spend almost the entire walk along the white cliffs of the Atlantic Ocean. On a clear day you will be able to see far into the ocean, experience great views of the cliffs, and watch the sunbathers on the beaches far below. When it is cloudy, visibility is poor. Although you will not see much, you will experience an edge-of-the-world loneliness and the sounds of ocean, wind, and sea gulls will be your constant companions.

Optional Maps/topo-guides: Série Bleu 1710 est/1809 ouest; GR 21 (reference #205) Falaises et Valleuses du Pays de Caux (pp. 22–23)

Time/Distance: 1 hour 45 minutes/5 miles (8 kilometers)

Difficulties: Two short but difficult climbs in both directions

Toilet Facilities: None except at Etretat; some privacy, but no forested areas and other hikers pass regularly

Refreshments: Only at Etretat

Getting There: Take the bus from Etretat to Vattetot-sur-Mer, which departs two or three times daily. You will emerge from the bus at the town center where you will see the *mairie* (town hall). Follow the road that the bus arrived on in the direction away from Etretat, past the church (also at the town center). Here you can turn right or left; either direction will take you to a sign that leads to the coast. If you go left, you will soon see a sign that indicates a right turn: "Chemin pour pietons 1.2 km." If you turn right, proceed just beyond the town where you will see a sign: "Les Falaises: chemin pour pietons 0.8 km." Turn left where you reach the coastal trail.

Trail Notes

___ 1. About twenty-five minutes into the walk, the trail will become impassable because of the heavy vegetation. Go beneath a barbed-wire fence directly to your left and descend through a field where you will pass under a gate that leads to a parking lot. After climbing under the gate, turn right, where you will see a waymark that will lead you uphill to the trail. (Throughout this entire trail you can walk on either side of the barbed wire fencing. I elected to stay closer to the ocean and never felt that I was too close to the cliffs.)

Suggestions for More Walking

Although the walk described above offers the best views of the Atlantic Ocean, the GR 21 trail stretches for 100 miles along the vicinity of the coast. However, most of the trail has been routed far enough into the interior to make ocean views uncommon. You may extend this walk by taking the same bus to Yport (total 6.5 miles) or Fecamp (total 10 miles). Another possibility is the attractive eight-mile interior walk that also includes some cliff walking from Gonneville-la-Mallet to Etretat. From Yport (78 miles) or Fécamp (75 miles) to Le Tréport there are numerous possibilities linked by public transportation.

Walk 4: Mont-Saint-Michel: Marvel of the West

Walk: Courtils to Mont-St-Michel

General Description

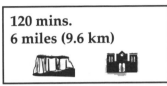

120 mins.
6 miles (9.6 km)

If you have ever seen a tourist brochure touting France's great attrac-
tions, you have seen a photograph of Mont-Saint-Michel, a.k.a.
the "marvel of the west." Truly one of the world's great sights,
the abbey church of Mont-Saint-Michel soars high above a precipitous, unadorned rock that becomes an island when it is enveloped by the fast flowing evening tide. Built in fortress style by
security-conscious monks, the "Mont" has withstood centuries of
assault by marauders, pilgrims, and now tourists.

According to legend, the Archangel Michael appeared in the
early eighth century to the Bishop of Avranches, who promptly
dedicated a small church to the saint. Numerous structures appeared on this site until the present Gothic church was constructed
in the thirteenth century. Very little medieval loneliness survives,
and at times it is almost impossible to breathe as you become
part of an undulating human wave being pushed inexorably along
the single medieval street to the crowning glory of the abbey.
However, it is also possible to arrive early and partake in the
solitary inspiration that this site demands.

Visit the abbey as the culmination of today's pilgrimage, retro-
experiencing the trials and tribulations of a medieval voyager. Take
the quick, not-quite-medieval bus ride to Courtils, a crumbling,
weather-beaten, but oddly attractive village that offers a range of
amenities including a church, a couple of rustic hotel/restaurants,
some greasy-spoon snack bars, and an inexpensive campground.
You will see Mont-Saint-Michel as only a few sheep and perhaps
their shepherds have seen it. Walking through Courtils and along

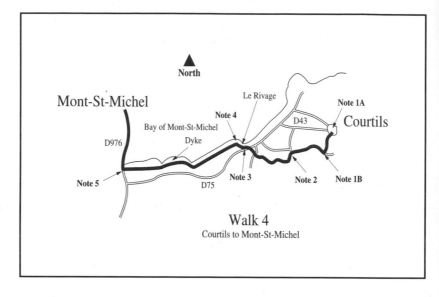

a series of seldom used rural tracks, you will soon reach the extensive bay of Mont-Saint-Michel. Paralleling protective dykes, you will be delighted by the pilgrim's-eye-view of the abbey's astonishing magnificence. Linger for a while at various points as the ever-varying vistas, often altered by Normandy's capricious weather patterns, create an immense and indelible psychological tableau.

Optional Maps/topo-guides: Série Bleu 1215 est; GR 223 (reference #200) Tour du Cotentin: Manche

Time/Distance: 2 hours/6 miles (9.6 kilometers)

Difficulties: None

Toilet Facilities: None, but much privacy

Refreshments: Courtils and Mont-Saint-Michel

Getting There: Buses (#12 Granville/Avranches/Le Mont-Saint-Michel) run every day during July and August, but slightly less frequently during other times of the year. The tourist office at Mont-Saint-Michel will be able to inform you, or call STN's office in Avranches (33 58 03 07). Inform the driver that you wish to get off at the "parking" where the toilets are located in Courtils.

Trail Notes

___ 1a. The bus will let you off across from the parking lot where the public toilets are located. Walk forward in the direction that the bus continues, and turn right at the first street; you will see a faded waymark.

___ 1b. Continue down this street past a crossroads until you hit a dead end, where you will turn right.

___ 2. When you hit the next dead end, turn left and follow this narrow asphalt band as it makes its way circuitously back to the main road D75.

___ 3a. When you reach D75 turn left, and you will soon see a parking lot/picnic ground called "Le Rivage."

___ 3b. At the far end of the parking lot, you will see the arrow that leads you through a gate (just unhook the chain from the nail on the post to get through) and down to the coast.

___ 4. You will quickly turn left at the fence and follow the raised earth called the dyke and fence back to the road that leads to Mont-Saint-Michel. Do not be tempted to make a bee-line back to Mont-Saint-Michel; you could be caught in the tides. As long as you stay along the fence/dyke you will be perfectly safe.

___ 5. The trail dead ends at the road that leads to Mont-Saint-Michel. Turn right and walk to the "Mont."

Suggestions for More Walking

For a shorter walk (about four miles), ask the driver to drop you off at Le Rivage and follow the directions starting at note 3b. You may also approach Mont-Saint-Michel from the other direction by taking the bus to Cherrueix and following the coastal trail about ten miles back to the "Mont."

Walk 5: Brittany: The Emerald Coast

Walk: St-Lunaire to St-Malo

General Description

120 mins.
6.2 miles (10 km)

Today's walk follows a serpentine six-mile path along the powerful waters of the Atlantic Ocean. This dazzling day begins at St-Malo, a former pirate haven, which was almost completely destroyed during the late stages of World War II. Inhabited not only by brigands, St-Malo was also the home of Jacques Cartier, who sailed from this city in 1534 to Canada, which he claimed for the king of France. The city and its walls have been completely restored to their pre-eighteenth-century appearance, and St-Malo's lively nightlife, elegant appearance, and comfortable, reasonably-priced accommodations make it an excellent base for exploring Brittany. After a day of walking and perhaps some carousing, stroll along the ramparts as evening approaches; as the sun drops slowly into the ocean, you will be greeted by one of the finest sunsets available to humankind.

A leisurely bus ride through sleepy resort/fishing villages will take you to St-Lunaire, where you can visit the eleventh-century church, explore seaside shops, dine, or perhaps go for a swim. Look far into the ocean and enjoy frequent views of St-Malo as the route back to the pirate town takes you along sandy beaches and rocky cliffs, passing the occasional WWII bunker, until you reach the elegant beach resort Dinard, just across the bay from St-Malo. Here, BCBGs (French yuppies) bake idly along the broad, sandy beaches, and a swift ferry will take you back to historic St-Malo.

Optional Maps/topo-guides: Série Bleu 1115 ouest; GR 34 (reference #310) Côte d'Emeraude: Mont-Saint-Michel/Saint-Brieuc

Time/Distance: 2 hours/6.2 miles (10 kilometers)

Difficulties: Frequent minor ups and downs

Toilet Facilities: At the beaches/some privacy

Refreshments: At the beaches

Getting There: T/V (Tourisme Vernay) buses depart several times per day from the Esplanade St-Vincent, platform 16 (Dinard, St-Briac, Ploubalay), which is directly outside of St-Malo's main gate. Information and schedules can be found at the T/V office also on the esplanade, or call 99 40 83 33. Ask the driver to let you off at the *office de tourisme* on the boulevard Charles de Gaulle.

Trail Notes

___ 1a. Walk back towards St-Malo on the boulevard Charles de Gaulle.

___ 1b. Quickly turn right on boulevard de la Plage, where you will soon see a waymark.

___ 1c. When you reach the main road (D786) on which the buses run, turn left.

___ 1d. Very quickly, a waymark points the way left and away from D786.

___ 2. When you come to the Plage (beach) de la Fourberie cross to the far side and rejoin the trail along the cliffs.

___ 3. When you quickly come to the next beach cross and rejoin the cliffs on the far side. (Important: during the summer of 1994, the cliff trail was blocked at this point because of the possibility of it crumbling. If it has not been repaired when you arrive here, walk away from the far side of the beach on an asphalt road (rue du Sergent Boulanger) and turn left on the rue Port Blanc at the end of the campground/park; you will see a sign "St-Enogat." Turn left at the second intersection; at the end of the street, you will see the rather large Institut Thallasotherapie and a stone wall to the left of the institute. Follow the wall to the coast and turn right. You will be back on the trail.)

___ 4. From this point, simply follow the coast into and around Dinard.

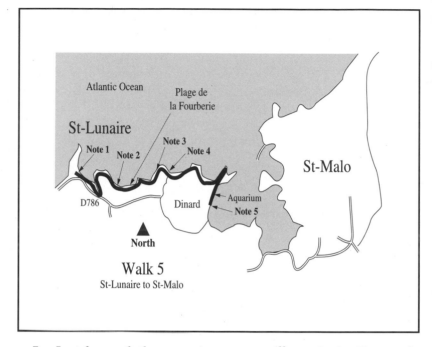

Atlantic Ocean

Plage de
la Fourberie

St-Lunaire

Note 1 Note 2 Note 3 Note 4

St-Malo

D786 Dinard Aquarium

Note 5

North

Walk 5
St-Lunaire to St-Malo

___ 5. Just beyond the aquarium, you will reach the Emeraude Lines office, where you can catch the water taxi back to St-Malo. (Occasionally the tide is not high enough to depart from this point. Look for a sign on the office; if you do not see your date and time of departure, walk back about ¹/₄-mile to the dock just below the Hôtel de la Vallée.) Alternatively, you can walk up to the center of town and take the bus back to St-Malo.

Suggestions for More Walking

In order to extend this walk by an extra five or seven miles continue on the bus to St-Briac or Lancieux and follow the spectacular coast back to St-Malo. A slightly shorter walk involves taking a local bus to Rotheneuf just east of St-Malo and walking five miles along the coast while passing the elegant mansions and hotels on the outskirts of the city.

Walk 6: Brittany's Wild Coast: Pointe du Grouin

Walk: **Cancale to Pointe du Grouin**

General description

105 mins.
5 miles (8 km)

Departing Cancale, which is renowned throughout France for its oyster cultivation and fine seafood, you will have fond memories of this gourmet's paradise. As you climb high from this friendly, scenic oceanside resort, you will observe the fertile oyster beds that stretch for miles into the ocean. Traversing the rocky trail, called the *Sentier des Douaniers* (trail of the customs agents) because it was formerly used by customs agents to intercept smugglers, you will marvel at some of the most rugged coastal scenery on the European continent. You will also be reminded, passing concrete bunkers erected by Nazis fearing Allied invasion, that only fifty years ago the world was at war, and France awaited liberation.

Pointe du Gruoin is celebrated for its views of the tempestuous Atlantic and its serrated coast. On a clear day, it is claimed that Mont-St-Michel can be seen. This is a popular walk. You will not be alone, but the unique, panoramic vistas are worth any inconvenience.

Optional Maps/topo-guides: Série Bleu 1215 ouest; GR 34 (reference #310) Côte d'Emeraude: Mont-Saint-Michel/Saint-Brieuc (pp. 28–31); Footpaths of Europe series: *Coastal Walks: Normandy and Brittany*

Time/Distance: 1 hour 45 minutes/5 miles (8 kilometers)

Difficulties: This rocky trail necessitates boots with firm soles, and the walking tends to be strenuous because of the frequent, although short, climbs and descents.

Toilet Facilities: About fifty-five minutes out of Cancale, near Port Briac, you will descend to sea level and cross a parking lot where there is a rest room. About fifteen minutes later, at a beach, you will find another rest room. At Port Mer and Pointe du Grouin there are also rest rooms.

Refreshments: There are cafés and restaurants at Port Mer and Pointe du Grouin.

Getting There: From Mont-St-Michel (27 miles) take D976 south to D797 west, which becomes D153. Turn right at D76, which takes you into Cancale. From St-Malo (9 miles), follow D953 to D355, which goes directly to Cancale. During July and August, three to four buses per day run between Cancale and Pointe du Grouin (schedules available at the tourist office, or telephone Les Couriers Bretons at 99 59 79 09 in St-Malo). During the rest of the year you will have to take a cab or walk both directions. In addition, both Tourisme Verney (tel. 99 40 82 670) and Les Couriers Bretons (tel. 99 56 79 09) offer service from St-Malo's bus station to Cancale. Be certain to check return times and walk with the speed necessary to avoid missing the last bus.

Trail Notes

___ 1. The trail simply follows the coast north from Cancale and is well marked and heavily travelled. You should have no trouble finding you way.

Suggestions for More Walking

This walk can be abbreviated to less than an hour by taking the bus to Port Briac instead of Cancale. Since buses run regularly along the coast between Cancale and St-Malo during July and August numerous spectacular walk combinations can be assembled. For example, you could leave your car at Le Verger, where there is a magnificent beach, take the bus to Cancale and walk back the astonishing eight miles from Cancale to your car. With a map and a bus schedule, the possibilities are endless.

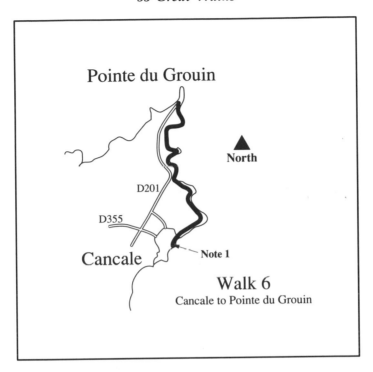

Pointe du Grouin

▲
North

D201

D355

Cancale — Note 1

Walk 6
Cancale to Pointe du Grouin

Walk 7: Brittany: Dol-de-Bretagne

Walk: Vivier-sur-Mer to Mont-Dol to Dol-de-Bretagne

105 mins.
5 miles (8 km)

General Description

Vivier-sur-Mer, attractively situated on Brittany's Atlantic coast, is a small village that offers all of the amenities expected in a resort area—a few hotels, several good restaurants, and great views of the ocean that extend as far as Pointe de Grouin and Mont-Saint-Michel. You may wish to linger here for lunch or a beverage before making the quick trek along the seaboard and then inland on your quest for mystical Mont-Dol.

En route, you will traverse an area of bucolic serenity punctuated by the weathered beauty of three traditional Breton hamlets. A quick aerobic climb to the summit of dwarfish Mont-Dol delivers you to a mythical plateau, site of a terrific struggle between the forces of good and evil. Here, according to legend, St. Michael hurled the Devil violently onto the rocky surface, and the Devil, in an attempt to break his fall, left a great claw mark on the hard granite that is still visible today. Then, with a single strike of his sword, Archangel Michael tore a gaping hole into the mountain where his Horniness was unceremoniously dumped. Wiley Satan, however, escaped only to reappear on Mont-Saint-Michel; Michael, in pursuit, reached the Devil in a single bound, leaving forever his footprint on Mont-Dol.

Mont-Dol was long ago inhabited by our fur-wearing ancestors and their unfortunate prey. Numerous stone and flint artifacts have been recovered as well as the remains of mammoths, reindeer, rhinoceros, and other prehistoric meals. Currently, the tiny chapel Notre-Dame-de-l'Espérance, complemented by a small hotel-restaurant, picnic grounds, toilets, windmills, and exceptional views in all directions, continues to be a popular pilgrimage site.

From Mont-Dol, Dol-de-Bretagne is in constant view, providing exceptional visual delight. Perched high upon a cliff, Dol-de-Bretagne clings zealously to its medival heritage. Dol's present obscurity belies its former significance as the seat of an influential bishop. A tour of the extraordinary, thirteenth-century Saint-Samson Cathedral will propel you through a time warp and into the city's former medieval magnificence, as will a stroll along the Promenade des Douves where you will be greeted by fine views of Mont-Dol and the surrounding countryside. From the promenade, descend to the city and inspect an excellent assemblage of centuries-old medieval structures. One of these structures houses an interesting museum dedicated to the storied past of Dol-de-Bretagne and the surrounding area.

Optional Maps/topo-guides: Série Bleu 1216 ouest; GR 34 (reference #310) Côte d'Emeraude: Mont-Saint-Michel/Saint-Brieuc

Time/Distance: 1 hour 45 minutes/5 miles (8 kilometers)

Difficulties: Short but aerobic climb up Mont-Dol

Toilet Facilities: Vivier-sur-Mer, Mont-Dol, Dol-de-Bretagne

Refreshments: Vivier-sur-Mer, Mont-Dol, Dol-de-Bretagne

Getting There: Buses for Vivier-sur-Mer leave Dol-de-Bretagne's train station, where the schedules are posted (there is also a bus stop and schedule at the post office), either early in the morning or late in the afternoon, but the walk is short and even if you take the late afternoon option it can be easily completed before darkness.

Trail Notes

___ 1a. From Vivier-sur-Mer, walk west (away from Mont-Saint-Michel) along the oceanfront dyke about one kilometer until you reach a large Citroën dealership that has an attached Glorex gas station.

___ 1b. Turn left at the narrow road (rue du Bord de Mer) adjacent to the Citroën dealership. You will see a waymark on a yield sign.

___ 2. From this point until the foot of Mont-Dol the trail is clearly marked and easy to follow.

___ 3. When you reach the foot of Mont-Dol you will see an arrow pointing left. As you walk in this direction, look to your right for an opening that leads upward. It may be quite overgrown but you will see a waymark on the tree. If you reach the red and white X on a telephone pole, go back and keep looking. You will find it.

___ 4. From Mont-Dol, the trail is clearly marked and easy to follow into Dol-de-Bretagne.

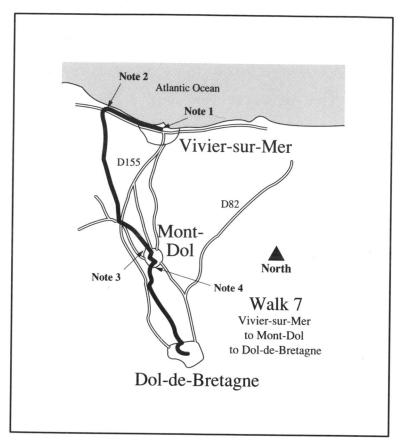

Suggestions for More Walking

You can extend this walk to about 11 miles (18 kilometers) by continuing on the same bus until you reach Cancale; the walk back to Dol-de-Bretagne is primarily along the coast and affords marvellous views. If you are in a hurry, try the 2.5-mile round trip from Dol-de-Bretagne to Mont-Dol—the views are excellent in both directions.

Walk 8: Loire Valley: Joan of Arc's Château

Walk: Hôpital Saint-Benoit-le-Forêt to Château Chinon

**120 mins.
5.5 miles (8.8 km)**

General Description

Exit from the bus and quickly enter the deep and verdant Forêt Domaniale de Chinon, formerly the hunting domain of nobility. Large stands of deciduous and coniferous trees cede only to the narrow band of earth that you will stride upon—savor the rustic tranquility. Emerging from the medieval forest and into the late twentieth century, you will amble through a recently constructed industrial zone—familiar looking but nonetheless clearly French in its execution. Note the interesting forms incorporated into the attractive and innovative structures of mundane use and also how it is less expensively accomplished by extensive use of colorful, corrugated steel facades. Such industrial zones and their concomitant suburbs signal France's imminent Americanization. Exit the industrial zone and pass into a tree-lined, shady path leading to extensive fields of shimmering wild flowers and renowned Chinon vineyards.

The entry into Chinon is one of the most interesting and scenic anywhere in Europe. As you approach Chinon, you will pass directly by numerous *maisons troglodytiques*, homes that have been carved into the chalky cliffs and finished through the addition of a stone facade. Some are still occupied and look quite comfortable; however, they are primarily the abodes of the impoverished. Nestled among the cave dwellings is Chapelle St-Radagonde, also partially carved into the rock during the eleventh and twelfth centuries, where you may wish to visit the associated museum illustrating the lives of the cave dwellers. Just before the entrance to the Château de Chinon, you will pass the Ancienne Eglise de St-

Martin, a church which has survived in various structures since the sixth century.

Château Chinon is one of the premier castles of the Loire Valley. Looming precipitously over the Vienne River, this venerable twelfth-century fortress is most famous as the setting for Joan of Arc's recognition of the disguised Charles VII among 300 richly attired noblemen in 1429. Joan and, eventually, the *château* itself fell on hard times; however, the *château* tour can still transport you back to those times of violent warfare between France and England. Stroll along the ramparts; explore interior chambers replete with wax figures; and inspect the exciting museum dedicated to Joan of Arc in the fifteenth-century bell tower above the castle gate.

After visiting the *château*, descend to the city and its narrow medieval corridors, which were known by the youthful Rabelais; tour the unique Musée du Vin where robo-vintners explain the wine-creating process in monotonic mechano-speech, including words of wisdom from Rabelais; and pass a quiet evening at a café in the town center. The entire Chinon experience is the essence of France.

Optional Maps/topo-guides: Série Bleu 1723 est; GR 3 (reference #303) Châteaux du Val de Loire

Time/Distance: 2 hours/5.5 miles (8.8 kilometers)

Difficulties: Some climbing, but not excessive

Toilet Facilities: None, but some privacy

Refreshments: Chinon

Getting There: Buses operated by SCNF leave the train station four times per day except Sundays and holidays, when there is only one bus. Schedules are available at the train station or tourist office. You will get off the bus at Hôpital St-Benoit-le-Forêt (which as its name implies is a hospital).

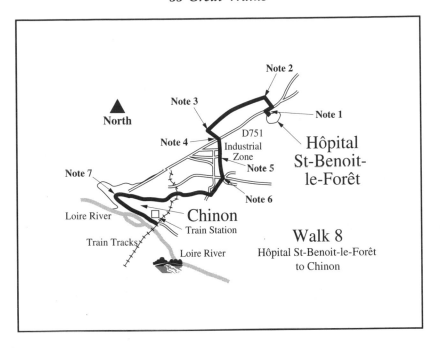

North

Note 2

Note 3

Note 1

Note 4

D751
Industrial Zone

Note 5

Note 7

Note 6

Loire River

Hôpital
St-Benoit-
le-Forêt

Chinon

Train Station

Train Tracks

Loire River

Walk 8

Hôpital St-Benoit-le-Forêt
to Chinon

Trail Notes

___ 1a. When you exit the bus, cross to the other side of the road and turn right.

___ 1b. Begin looking to your left. After a couple of minutes, you will see a narrow asphalt road identified by a sign as "Route du Louis XI." There is also a large house at the side of this road. Walk down this road into the forest.

___ 2. After about five minutes you will turn left onto a wide dirt path identified by a horse path sign and also a waymark. From this point the trail is well marked and easy to follow.

___ 3. When you come to the first vehicular road turn left; it is clearly marked.

___ 4. When you reach D751 (the road the bus took you on) continue straight and cross the road. It is clearly marked.

___ 5. After a few minutes in the industrial zone, watch carefully for a right and then quick left onto a wide dirt track; it is well marked but can be missed if you are inattentive.

___ 6. After passing through the vineyards, you will turn left on an asphalt road and then quickly right. Both turns are clearly marked. From this point, the trail is clearly marked, but watch for waymarks and X's.

___ 7. When you descend into the city take either the riverside street to the left or the street just before it to the left in order to return to the railroad station.

Suggestions for More Walking

For a very long 17-mile walk take the same bus to Azay-le-Rideau, visit the great *château* and walk back along the trail GR 3 to Chinon. There is no possibility of a shorter variation of this walk using public transportation; however, for a shorter jaunt, you could take the tourist steam train in the direction of Richelieu to the first stop (Ligre-Rivière); walk into the town of Rivière along a seldom-used secondary road; and follow the riverside path to D749 where you can cross the bridge into Chinon (total of about 3.5 miles).

Walk 9: Loire Valley: Elegant Chenonceau

Walk: La Croix-en-Touraine to Château de Chenonceau

105 mins.
5.5 miles (8.8 km)

General Description

Bléré, ensconced on the tranquil banks of the Cher River, lingers obscurely in the long tourist shadow cast by its super-nova neighbor Chenonceau. Obscurity aside, Bléré is a worthy place to sojourn while *château*-hopping in the region—

typically French, pleasantly situated along the Cher River, and just enough commerce to keep you from being homeless and hungry.

Walk out of town and along the lovely banks of the Cher to Chenonceau. You will never lose site of this serene waterway as you traverse fields, suburbia, and finally a sylvan paradise en route to France's most elegant *château*.

Chenonceau, which gracefully spans the Cher, seems to float on rather than be anchored in this lovely river; when the water is still, it is often difficult to distinguish the shimmering reflection from the *château* itself. Constructed during the sixteenth century, the refined architecture of Chenonceau reflects the aesthetic predilections of the women who dominated this *château*. Catherine Briconnet, wife of busy finance minister Thomas Bohier, controlled the construction of the *château* while her husband sorted out affairs of state. Later, young Henry II gave Chenonceau to his slightly older and most beautiful lover, Diane de Poitiers, who added the extensive gardens. After Henry's death, his queen Catherine de

Medici forced Diane to exchange Chenonceau for the gloomy Château Chaumont. Catherine was responsible for the construction of Chenonceau's signature galleries that span the Cher.

You will literally enter Chenonceau through the back door and cross over the river through the lower gallery, which offers wonderful views and, on a hot day, cool breezes. If you have not seen the *château* before, save yourself for this approach which is much more aesthetically pleasing than the view from the main gate where drivers and tourist bus passengers enter.

Optional Maps/topo-guides: Série Bleu 1923 est & 2023 ouest; GR 41

Time/Distance: 1 hour 45 minutes/5.5 miles (8.8 kilometers)

Difficulties: None

Toilet Facilities: None, but some privacy

Refreshments: None

Getting There: Trains (four per day except Sunday when there is only one) leave the Chenonceau-Chisseaux station, which is about one mile east of the town Chenonceau at the junction of D40 and D80. You will get off at the Bléré-la-Croix station, which is either the first or second stop depending on the time that you take the train. These stops are on the Tours/Vierzon line, so you can comfortably make the city of Tours your base if you do not have a car. There are, however, hotels at Bléré, Chenonceau, and nearby Amboise.

Trail Notes

___ 1. From the train station, walk east to the road (D31 avenue du Chere, the only road in the vicinity), turn right and walk into Bléré.

___ 2. When you cross the bridge over the Cher River (you will be in Bléré) turn left and follow the path along the river. You will be on this path for the duration of this walk.

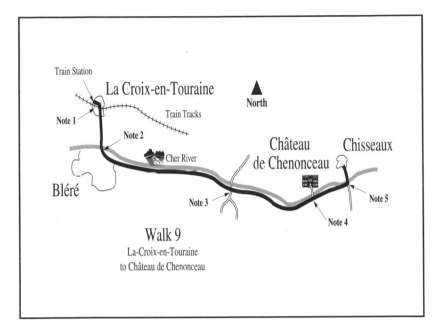

La Croix-en-Touraine

Train Station

Note 1

Train Tracks

North

Note 2

Cher River

Château
de Chenonceau

Chisseaux

Blére

Note 3

Note 5

Note 4

Walk 9

La-Croix-en-Touraine
to Château de Chenonceau

___ 3. When you get to the first traffic bridge ignore the red and white X and continue under the bridge along the Cher. (The best views are on this side)

___ 4. When you reach Chenonceau, you can literally enter through the back door in order to visit the *château.*

___ 5. After you have visited the *château,* continue down the trail to the first bridge where you turn left and walk up to the train station.

Suggestions for More Walking

For a slightly longer walk (7.5 miles), leave your car at the same station but take the train to Chissay-en-Touraine in the opposite direction and walk back to the station via an attractive rural/ forest walk. For another, longer, variation (about 10 miles) take the train to the stop past Bléré-la-Croix at St-Martin-le-Beau, cross the river near a place called Chandon, and follow the Cher back to Chenonceau.

Walk 10: In the Land of Early Man: Les Eyzies-de-Tayac

Walk: Le Bugue to Les Eyzies-de-Tayac

**165 mins.
8.2 miles (13.2 km)**

General Description

This is a long but eventful walk as you walk high in the land of early man. Lively little Le Bugue, your starting point, is a charming community that hangs on the banks of the Vézère River. Hotels, restaurants, and all other forms of commerce are available here, making it an attractive off-the-beaten path pause. About a half mile northwest of the town is located the well-known Grotte (cave) of Bara-Bahau, housing a collection of interesting prehistoric animal drawings; and about two miles south of town lies the Gouffre (abyss) de Proumeyssac, where you can explore an underground passage replete with multi-colored stalagmites.

Climbing out of Le Bugue along a cheery country lane, you will quickly pass through a series of fields while enjoying excellent views of the Vézère River and its valley in the distance. Fields surrender to forest as you take a circuitous route, via the rustic hamlet called La Peyrière, to St-Cirq and the famous Grotte (cave) du Sorcier, renowned for its excellent prehistoric drawings. Near the cave entrance are a series of engravings and some sculptural remains; near the back are other engravings, including one of a man called the Sorcerer. This particular engraving is considered to be one of the finest known from the prehistoric period. Relax at the cave entrance and contemplate the passage of time.

Departing St-Cirq and still trekking loftily in the country of our early ancestors, you will pass through a primeval forest punctuated by a series of stunning vistas. Close to Les Eyzies, you will encounter the Gorge d'Enfer (Hell's Canyon), an interesting site of early human habitation and worth a quick stop. You will also come upon the Musée Speliologie, located deep in a high cliff overlooking Les Eyzies and containing a variety of exhibits relating to caves and their exploration.

Les Eyzies, one of the great centers of early human discovery, is the home of two excellent museums and a center for prehistoric cave exploration. The Musée National de Préhistoire, located in the cliffs above the town center, has an extensive collection of early human artifacts and art works, while the Musée L'Abri Pataud is constructed around excavations revealing more than a dozen levels of human habitation. It also houses a video display explaining evolution and prehistory. Just beyond the town limits lies the Grotte de Font-de-Gaume, which harbors twenty-thousand-year-old drawings of such extinct creatures as mammoths and early versions of reindeer, bison, and horses. The paintings, although faded, are remarkable for their sophistication and naturalistic appearance. Also noteworthy for numerous etchings of early game animals is the Grotte des Combarelles, which is about a mile down D47 from the Grotte de Font-de-Gaume. Numerous other caves abound in the general area and the tourist office will give you a comprehensive list.

In addition to hiking, museum visiting, and cave exploring, you may wish to float down the Vézère and Dordogne rivers; there are several places in town that offer canoe and kayak rental.

Optional Maps/topo-guides: Série Bleu 1936 est; GR 36/6 (reference #359) Périgord Quercy: Monbazillac/Les Eyzies/Cahors

Time/Distance: 2 hours 45 minutes/8.2 miles (13.2 kilometers)

Difficulties: Two climbs of 15 and 10 minutes, and several other short climbs

Toilet Facilities: None

Refreshments: None between towns

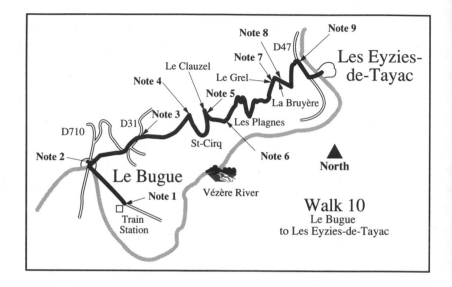

Note 8
Note 9
D47
Note 7
Le Clauzel
Le Grel
Les Eyzies-de-Tayac
Note 4
Note 5
Note 3
La Bruyère
D31
D710
Les Plagnes
St-Cirq
Note 2
Note 6
North
Le Bugue
Note 1
Vézère River
Train Station

Walk 10
Le Bugue
to Les Eyzies-de-Tayac

Getting There: Trains run several times daily to Le Bugue, which is the first stop from Les Eyzies. The schedule is posted on the door of the train station and inside. Your train and time of departure is the one in the direction of Agen. The train arrives on the station side of the platform.

Trail Notes

Note: Some of the waymarks will be red, white, and orange, since this is both a *grande randonée* and a *petite randonée*.

___ 1.   From the station, walk to the road, turn left and walk twenty minutes into the center of town.

___ 2a. When you reach the town center, which is a square into which a bridge over the Vézère feeds traffic, turn right and climb a short broad staircase.

___ 2b. Turn right again at the top of the stairs onto a narrow asphalt street. You are on the trail and will soon see a waymark.

__ 3. When you reach a sign that indicates "Petit Paris/La Péyriere," turn right. The waymarks are visible but there is no change-direction waymark.

__ 4. When you reach Suscanaval, go right. The trail is marked but you must pay attention.

__ 5. At Clauzel you will turn right at the sign that indicates "Les Plagnes/La Raysse." It is marked but faded.

__ 6. At Les Plagnes, look left; it's marked but easy to miss.

__ 7. At Le Grel, when you see the *"passage interdite"* ("no entry") sign, go left along the fence. It is waymarked.

__ 8. Just past La Bruyère, where you see the sign "La Barbarie" leading left, go directly right where you see a yellow arrow and continue downhill. You will soon see a red and white waymark.

__ 9. When you come to the vehicular road leading to Les Eyzies, cross to the other side and go right along the pedestrian path into the town.

Suggestions for More Walking

There is no possibility of lengthening or shortening this walk using public transportation. However, for a very long (about 17 miles) but magnificent day's journey into night try the tiring trek from medieval Sarlat-la-Canéda to Les Eyzies. Two to three buses per day with a change at Le Buisson run between these two venerable tourist sites.

Walk 11: In the Land of Early Man: Lascaux/Montignac

Walk: Route de St-Amand-de-Coly to Lascaux/Montignac

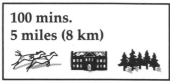

100 mins.
5 miles (8 km)

General Description

Within minutes of embarking upon today's adventure, the Château de Filolie, a remarkable site set in a pristine valley, comes into view. It is not often that you will be able to pass almost directly through a working, inhabited *château*, and this enormous edifice with its associated buildings is in magnificent condition. In spite of the euphoria associated with this opportunity I couldn't avoid thinking about the plumbing, the electricity, and the cost of heat, which probably add up to my yearly income. Avoid such mundane thoughts as you pass around and directly through the *château* complex. Take your time and enjoy this rare opportunity.

Passing through the valley and into the high country, beautiful vistas abound throughout this lovely, forested walk. Not far from Lascaux, you will come upon the site of Regourdou, where, in 1957, the almost complete skeleton of a 70,000-year-old Neanderthal man was found with the remains of a number of bears, which has led to speculation of an early cult dedicated to these shaggy beasts. The site is open to tourists and there is also, unfortunately, a live bear exhibit.

Lascaux, just before Montignac, is one of the world's most renowned prehistoric caves. Discovered in 1940 by a group of surprised teenagers, Lascaux was open to the general public until the early sixties when it had to be closed because humidity from human breathing was causing the 17,000-year-old drawings to deteriorate. The French government, not wanting to lose one of its premier tourist attractions, constructed an exact replica of Lascaux creatively named Lascaux II (the sequel?), where ancient deer and buffalo roam unmolested along craggy cave walls. Purchase tickets for this crowded but not-to-be-missed site at the Montignac tourist office before you hit the trail.

The final approach from Lascaux II to Montignac is quite pleasant as you make a swift transition from forestland to pasture land to city hinterland and finally into the center of bustling Montignac. This popular tourist center, tightly packed along the banks of the Vézère River, is a pleasant overnight stop where you can stroll along river banks and through narrow lanes, perhaps renting a canoe or kayak for a float down the Vézère River.

Optional Maps/topo-guides: Série Bleue 2035 ouest; GR 36/436/461 (reference #356) Périgord: Découverte de la Préhistoire

Time/Distance: 1 hour 40 minutes/5 miles (8 kilometers)

Difficulties: Several short climbs

Toilet Facilities: Lascaux, some privacy

Refreshments: Restaurant Belle Vue (you can dine on the terrace, which has expansive views of Montignac and the surrounding territory) just before Lascaux; snack bar at Lascaux

Getting There: During July and August there are usually two buses per day from Montignac to St-Amand-de-Coly, one in the morning and one in the evening. During other times of the year there is only an evening bus. Given the fact that it does not become dark until 10:00 p.m. in June, it is possible to do this as an evening stroll. However, it is preferable to take a taxi to the starting point since it is a short drive and will not cost too much. If you take a taxi, go to the office of Michel Rougerie at the place de Tourny just east of the tourist office at Montignac. They employ a number of drivers and can have one at your disposal quickly. You can call ahead for a reservation at 53 51 97 20. (Other taxis: Taxi Saulière 53 50 86 61 and Taxi Loridan 53 51 82 20). The tourist office can

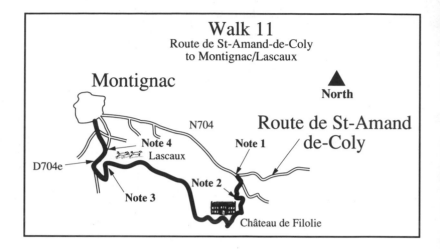

Walk 11

Route de St-Amand-de-Coly
to Montignac/Lascaux

Montignac

North

N704

Note 4

Lascaux

Route de St-Amand
de-Coly

Note 1

D704e

Note 2

Note 3

Château de Filolie

call for you. Simply show the bus or taxi driver the map. They will know where to deliver you.

Trail Notes

___ 1. From the bus stop near the road to St-Amand-de-Coly, walk directly ahead, you will see a waymark that will lead you down a road to the right.

___ 2. When you reach a wire fence that surrounds the Château de Filolie go left and follow the fence. From this point the trail is well marked and easy to follow until just beyond Lascaux. Watch for the waymarks and X's, and you will have no problem.

___ 3. Just beyond Lascaux, you will reach D704e, where you turn left and will soon begin to see waymarks again.

___ 4. Turn left at the arrow when you see the sign Puy Robert that directs you into town. When you reach the main street in Montignac, look left and you will see the tourist office.

Suggestions for More Walking

To extend this walk, have a taxi driver (no buses go to this remote town) take you to the remarkable church of St-Amand-de-Coly, whose enormity and powerful fortifications are astonishing in such a remote location. The explanation lies in its function as a pilgrimage stop on the way to Santiago de Compostela. It is a beautiful site and worth the three extra miles. There is no possibiliy of shortening this walk with public transportation, but for a short, pleasant stroll, walk from Montignac to Lascaux II and back along the same trail.

Walk 12: Lovely Lot Valley: Cahors

Walk: **Douelle to Cahors**

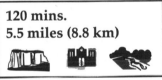

120 mins.
5.5 miles (8.8 km)

General Description

Douelle is a typical, unpretentious agricultural center. Here there are no monuments, but you can watch the time-honored structures of daily life in the forgotten France unfurl in slow motion. Tractors roll slowly through the main street disturbing no one; children play unhindered by urban dangers; and shopkeepers, conserving energy, await customers in the shadows. Stroll through this pleasant town and up into the stratosphere—the walk out of Douelle is very strenuous but offers remarkable views of the fertile Lot Valley and distant hill country. Do not scramble quickly up the hill—take your time and savor the stunning panorama.

After the initial climb, you will walk high along hill tops amidst multi-directional vanishing points. Distant vistas beckon, and soon you will reach a cliff top worshipped by hang gliders who risk life and limb for a quick glide over the Lot River. There is also a large cross in the vicinity, which I assume needs no explanation. As you approach Cahors, through this undulating arcadia, lovely

ANCIEN
HOPITAL DE GROSSIA
1270

stone fences grace your way. Constructed by early farmers who had nothing else to do with the stones that occupied their fields in droves, these fences find their origin in practicality but now provide profound aesthetic delight. Traversing ubiquitous fields, you will also pass occasional mansions constructed in a variety of styles and offering engaging architectural diversions.

Just before Cahors, you will begin to see the famous and impressive fortified bridge, Pont Valentré, which is the best preserved in all of Europe. Constructed in the fourteenth century, this venerable span has protected Cahors for hundreds of years and continues to stand solidly above the swift-moving Lot River.

Cahors, with its Spanish-influenced architecture and ubiquitous red-tiled roofs, juts colorfully into the surrounding fields and forests, presenting a striking vista. Almost completely surrounded by a loop in the Lot River, Cahors, with its narrow, medieval streets, comfortable accommodations, and fine food including the excellent vegetarian restaurant l'Orangerie, is an inviting summer retreat from the crowds. Inspect Pont Valentré; tour the fourteenth-century, Byzantine-inspired Cathédrale St-Etienne; wander along well-preserved medieval corridors; and delight in the immense market places. Cahors and the surrounding countryside are among France's most accommodating regions.

Optional Maps/topo-guides: Série Bleu 2038 est/2039 est; GR 36/6 (reference #359) Perigord Quercy: Monbazillac/Les Eyzies/Cahors

Time/Distance: 2 hours/5.5 miles (8.8 kilometers)

Difficulties: One strenuous 15-minute climb out of Douelle and one less strenuous 10-minute climb about midway

Toilet Facilities: None, but much privacy

Refreshments: None between towns

Getting There: Take the bus (route: Cahors to Monsempron-Libos) from the train station in Cahors. As you face the station, the bus

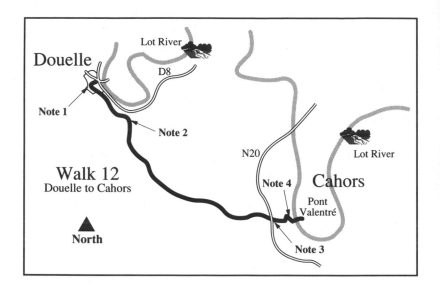

Lot River

Douelle

D8

Note 1

Note 2

N20

Lot River

Walk 12
Douelle to Cahors

Note 4

Cahors

Pont
Valentré

▲
North

Note 3

stop is to the far right, where you will also see a schedule. Purchase your ticket in the station. There are several buses daily. The bus will drop you off in the center of Douelle.

Trail Notes

___ 1a. As soon as the bus crosses the bridge over the Lot River, it turns right and drops you off immediately in the town square.

___ 1b. Directly across from the bridge is a school, which you will walk beyond to the left (straight ahead from the bridge).

___ 1c. One block later you will reach the *mairie* (town hall). Turn left here and walk toward the church. As you pass the church, you will see a red and white waymark.

___ 2a. When you reach the top of the climb out of Douelle, you will be by a large antenna.

___ 2b. Continue straight from the antenna until you see a large cross. (If you notice waymarks to your right, ignore them until you see the cross.)

___ 2c. Just before you reach the cross, there is a waymark on a rock on the ground here that leads to the right, and in the distance you will see a waymark on a utility pole to your right as you face the cross (do not continue to walk beyond the cross along the cliffs). From this waymark continue to follow the waymarks and X's.

___ 3. Near Cahors, you will cross under an enormous highway bridge (N20). Begin to look to your right for a rocky path that descends. It is marked and the wrong way has two X's on a low metal fence. Be alert.

___ 4a. The waymarks take you to the medieval fortified bridge Pont Valentré, where you turn left, cross the Lot River, and enter Cahors.

___ 4b. Continue straight from the bridge and quickly through a tunnel beneath the railroad tracks.

___ 4c. After emerging from the tunnel, walk to the first street, turn left, and you will be soon back at the train station.

Suggestions for More Walking

There are numerous walking opportunities along this portion of the Lot River that coincide with public transportation. The entire twenty-four mile trail between Puy-l'Evêque and Cahors consists of some of the finest walking in France. The same bus stops at Douelle, Luzech, Castelfranc, Prayssac, and Puy-l'Evêque. The ten miles between Castelfranc and Luzech are particularly eventful, starting at a thirteenth-century *donjon*, passing the hill-top Impernal where Julius Caesar defeated a large contingent of Gauls 2000 years ago, traversing stately Prayssac, and terminating at historic Castelfranc.

Walk 13: A Walk up the Rock: St-Cirque-la-Popie

Walk: Bouzies to St-Cirque-la-Popie to Tour de Faure

**80 mins.
3.6 miles (5.8 km)**

General Description

This short walk will take you along the banks of and under the steep cliffs that conceal the placid, slow-moving Lot River. Leaving the river, you will make a short but precipitous climb to St-Cirque-la-Popie, where you will enjoy an expansive view of the Lot and environs from the ruined *château* which looms 250 feet above the river. This highly defensible position has been successfully maintained against numerous invaders, and even thwarted the efforts of Richard the Lion Hearted to seize it in 1198. You will have the opportunity to explore this diminutive but renowned redoubt, which rivals, in its rugged fastness, Rocamadour. Wander the narrow streets and marvel at the ancient homes now mostly restored by artists and writers (the Surrealist writer/guru André Breton once lived here), enchanted by the region's ethereal charm. Visit the fifteenth-century church; climb to the formidable Château del Gardette; and relax over an expensive lunch or drink before making the easy descent to Tour de Faure where your car or the bus stop is waiting.

Optional Maps/topo-guides: Série Bleu 2138 est; GR 36/46 (reference #322) Cahors-Albi-Lot Aveyron

Time/Distance: 1 hour 20 minutes/3.6 miles (5.8 kilometers)

Difficulties: One steep climb

Toilet Facilities: Tourist office at St-Cirque-la-Popie

Refreshments: Cafés and restaurants at Bouzies and St-Cirque-la-Popie; also a store/café at the camp ground just before Tour de Faure

Getting There: From Cahors, drive to Tour de Faure (20 miles) via D653 and then D662. You will stop just before entering the village at the road that leads to St-Cirque-la-Popie. You can park on the road behind what was formerly the small train station but is now a private residence. You will also see an almost-new hotel along this road. From here walk back to the bus stop on D662 and take the eight-minute bus ride (4–5 per day; schedule "Ligne de Cahors-Figeac-Capdenac" can be obtained at the Cahors train station and should be posted at all stops) back to Bouzies (pont). Be certain to signal the bus driver since almost all stops on this line are optional.

From Cahors, via public transportation, take the bus from the train station to Bouzies (pont), where you will commence walking. You can take the bus back from Tour de Faure (schedules at the Cahors train station).

Trail Notes

___ 1a. From the Bouzies (pont) bus stop walk over the bridge to Bouzies.

___ 1b. As soon as you cross the bridge, make a sharp right which will take you beside the bridge back in the direction of the bus stop.

___ 1c. When you reach the river, turn right again and follow the river. The trail is clearly marked here but be certain that you are walking in the direction of St-Cirque-la-Popie and not Cahors.

___ 2. The remainder of the route is clearly marked into St-Cirque-la-Popie. You will first follow the river and then the canal. Soon after the canal and river rejoin, you will turn right and begin the ascent to St-Cirque-la-Popie.

___ 3. Departing from St-Cirque-la-Popie, you can ignore the

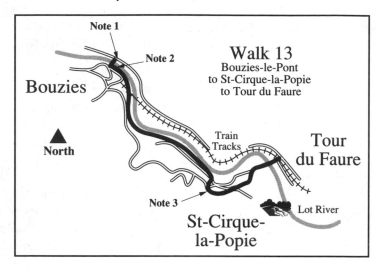

waymarks and walk down the only road that descends from the town, which will take you to Tour de Faure.

Suggestions for More Walking

This walk can be extended by taking the same bus to the Pont de St-Géry, where you can join the trail across the river. For other walks in the region see the Suggestions for More Walking in the above section about Cahors.

Walk 14: Along the Great Pilgrimage Trail: Moissac

Walk: Castelsarrasin to Moissac

General Description

Castelsarrasin, an ancient city that still conserves a few vestiges of its past,

**105 mins.
5 miles (8 km)**

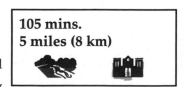

provides the walker with a amiable point of departure. Visit the thirteenth-century church; roam about the town inspecting the occasional medieval home; and have a beverage pause in this relaxed, pleasant ambience before you stroll down the canal to medieval Moissac.

The nineteenth-century canal towpath and accompanying waterway serve as an extended park for residents along its entire length. People fish, picnic, play games, jog, cycle, and walk along the path, while the canal itself is a haven for pleasure cruisers. Just beyond the town, you will pass a typical above-ground cemetery skirting the canal; look to the rear and into the past as the grave markers become progressively older. You will also pass a number of aging factories that indicate the industrial nature of canals; they were constructed long ago for trade and commerce without the foresight to know that their ultimate use would be recreational.

Walking along the towpath, formerly trodden by countless beasts of burden towing weighty barges, you will pass numerous locks; each lock is accompanied by a lock-keeper's house. All of the houses have been creatively adorned with an effusion of flowers, and there appears to be a beautification competition that benefits all who traverse this charming canal.

Watch to your left about an hour out of Castelsarrasin for the Motel/Restaurant Félix, whose Wild West decor appears to have been inspired by a B-grade Hollywood set designer. Rooms come in the shape of teepees, mission churches, stage coach offices, saloons, etc. The menu reflects the general Old West theme, and Americans lonely for home-style food will adore this unique cultural landmark.

A literal high point occurs when the canal bridges, at great heights, the expanse of the River Tarn. This nineteenth-century engineering feat allows you to walk along a towpath elevated over another body of water and provides astonishing views in all directions.

Moissac, a major stop on the medieval pilgrimage trail to Santiago

de Compostela in Spain, radiates gently from the banks of the Tarn River and provides an intimate frame for the profoundly medieval abbey that provides the focal point and raison d'être for this otherwise obscure but attractive town.

Cloister lovers will delight in the other-worldly atmosphere of the magnificent cloister of the Abbaye de Moissac. Here you may weave casually in serpentine fashion around the dozens of famous columns whose capitals depict saintly lives and Old Testament terrors. This eleventh-century Romanesque masterpiece was widely imitated throughout Europe during the twelfth century and is a must-see on any twentieth-century tour of France.

Optional Maps/topo-guides: Série Bleu 1941 est; GR 65 (reference #613) Sentier de Saint-Jacques

Time/Distance: 1 hour 45 minutes/5 miles (8 kilometers)

Difficulties: None

Toilet Facilities: None between towns, some privacy

Refreshments: At the Motel/Restaurant Félix about 40 minutes before Moissac

Getting There: Trains to Castelsarrasin depart from the station at
Moissac on a regular basis. The train, direction Toulouse, departs
on the opposite side from the station.

Trail Notes

Note: There are no waymarks on this trail, but it is impossible to
become lost.

___ 1a. At Castelsarrasin, walk through the station, exiting on the
other side.

___ 1b. As you exit the station you will see a pedestrian bridge
over the canal. Cross the bridge and turn right along the
path that parallels the canal. You will follow this path all
the way into Moissac.

___ 2a. When you reach central Moissac, you will leave the canal
at the first traffic bridge that forces you up to the road
and turn right. (To your right, you will see the Gendarmerie Nationale and the route you ascend to is N113.)

___ 2b. Walk up two blocks and turn left where you dead end
and see a sign "gare S.N.C.F." You will soon be at the train
station.

Suggestions for More Walking

There is no possibility of lengthening or shortening this walk while
using public transportation. However, buses go to the hamlet
Durfort-Lacapelette north of Moissac, where you can join the GR
65 trail and hike the thirteen pilgrimage miles back to Moissac.

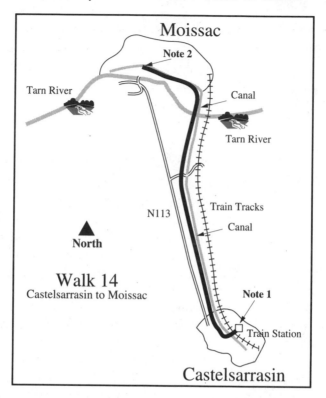

Moissac

Note 2

Tarn River

Canal

Tarn River

Train Tracks

Canal

N113

▲
North

Walk 14
Castelsarrasin to Moissac

Note 1

Train Station

Castelsarrasin

Walk 15: Carcassonne: Disney Castle

Walk: Conques-sur-Orbeil to Carcassonne

**110 mins.
5 miles (8 km)**

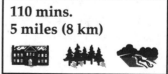

General Description

Rejoice in the astonishing view of distant Carcassonne as you set out on this medieval trek. It is an experience similar to spying Camelot, or perhaps even Oz, in the distance and knowing that great adventure awaits in a remote and mysterious citadel. As you gaze upon Carcassonne sprawling along the horizon, it is not hard to understand why Euro Disney (near Paris) has failed to capture European imaginations—they live in a fairy-tale landscape and Carcassonne is one of the finest sights in this magical landscape.

You will begin along a trail lined with fragrant coniferous trees on one side and abundant vineyards on the other. After traversing field and forest, you will follow the circuitous route of the famous Canal du Midi, which links the Atlantic Ocean with the Mediterranean Sea, into Carcassonne. You are also taking part in a truly international experience since the GR 36 trail you are on is also E (European hiking route) 4, which traverses several nations en route to Spain. As you walk along the canal with its interesting series of locks, Carcassonne is often in view, sometimes disappearing only to reappear again as you approach the castle.

Carcassonne is one of France's premier sites and was the setting for the recent swashbuckling Robin Hood film. Characterized by double-walled, medieval splendor, this most striking of European castles started its career as a pre-Christian, hill-top stronghold and has been fortified ever since. The current fortifications were erected during the thirteenth century, and incorporated the latest innovations in castle-building techniques from the Holy Lands where Frankish Crusaders, who were doused with more than their fair share of boiling oil, learned about the difficulties of assaulting double-walled citadels. Now surrounded by a modern commercial city, the *château* bustles with tourists whose ubiquity is sometimes more offensive than a mob of unwashed medieval besiegers. There is, however, no excuse for missing this carnival-disguised-as-history.

Optional Maps/topo-guides: Série Bleu 2345 est/2445 ouest; GR 36 (reference #348) Horizons des Pays d'Oc: Albi-Canigou

Time/Distance: 1 hour 50 minutes/5 miles (8 kilometers). Note: If you start at the Renault dealer you will subtract 20 minutes. If you elect to walk to the *château* rather than the railroad station, add 15 minutes.

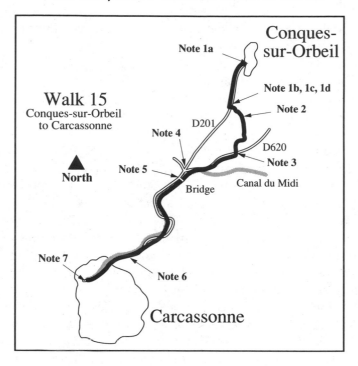

Difficulties: About 40 minutes of road walking (twenty minutes if you begin at the Renault dealership)

Toilet Facilities: None between towns, some privacy

Refreshments: None between towns

Getting There: Buses depart for Conques-sur-Orbeil from the bus stop directly across from the train station in Carcassonne in a small park called Jardin Chenier. The stop is right next to the small office of Transports Teissiers located in the park closest to the train station. There are 2–4 buses per day except Sundays. Schedule information is available at the tourist offices or at the Teissier office (tel. 68 25 85 45). If you wish to eliminate the walk back along D201 from Conques-sur-Orbeil ask the driver to let you off at the Renault repair facility just before Conques and NOT the Renault dealership just beyond Carcassonne, which is in a heavily developed area and across the street from a Honda dealer (say: *"chez Renault juste avant la ville de Conques"*).

Trail Notes

__ 1a. If you get off at the town, walk directly back down D201 (the road that the bus took you on) toward Carcassonne. When you get to the Renault facility (it is large and cannot be missed) begin to look left.

__ 1b. Continue down D201; just past Renault (do not turn left down the gravel road next to Renault), there is a new house. When you get to the end of the fence that encloses the house, you will see a small, probably overgrown, path that you turn left on, following the fence behind the house (recent construction has eliminated the waymark).

__ 1c. While walking along the fence, look to the right. You will see a waymark on a concrete utility pole not too far in the distance. Make your way through the small, overgrown field to this waymark.

__ 1d. Turn left when you get to the waymark and continue down this narrow asphalt road.

__ 2. When you quickly come to another narrow asphalt road, turn right and walk to the first house; it is surrounded by a large cinderblock fence, and there is a waymark on the wall. Go left along this fence. (Note: If there is no mark when you arrive here go left anyway since the fence still needs to be stuccoed, which will probably eliminate the waymark.)

__ 3. When you come to a vehicular road (D620), cross to the other side, turn right, and continue in the direction of Carcassonne. (This is an unpleasant twenty-minute walk but it shows how increasing urbanization is affecting France when there is no alternative but to walk down a heavily trafficked road.)

___ 4. When you come to a large traffic circle, continue to your left around the circle and turn left at the first road (there is no waymark because of recent construction).

___ 5. Look to your left as you walk down this road; you will soon see a small bridge over the Canal du Midi. Cross the bridge and turn right along the canal towpath that will lead you back to Carcassonne's train station.

___ 6. The orange arrows will take you back to the castle, but I advise you to bring a city map if you leave the canal at this point.

___ 7. From the train station, either use your city map to guide you to the castle or take the #4 bus.

Suggestions for More Walking

It is impossible to lengthen this walk via public transportation unless you are a strong swimmer; beyond Conques the trail and the bus are along opposite banks of the river, and there are no bridges. For a long day's walk (about 11 miles), you may wish to walk in a southerly direction from Carcassonne's *château* to Montirat and back (same topo-guide and maps). Take plenty of water and watch the path carefully because it is not always well marked.

Walk 16: Parc National des Cévennes: Land of Robert Louis Stevenson and his Donkey

Walk: Gare de Prévenchères to Villefort

220 mins.
9.5 miles (15.2 km)

General Description

This is the longest walk (dare we say trek) in the book, but you are in a region of great natural beauty that calls for, even demands, hearty outdoor ruggedness. The walk's the thing here, and you will not be disappointed. This is the land where Robert Louis Stevenson recorded his perambulations in *Travels with a Donkey in the Cévennes*. Now a travel classic, this 1878 donkey book was Stevenson's first big hit and you will traverse this unaltered landscape much in the same way that R. L. S. did, minus the mule (I was unable to locate a rent-an-ass agency).

Start at an abandoned train station (gare de Prévenchères) that looks like it could be a set for a spaghetti western. After circling the train station and visualizing a bustling but lost past, ascend to a high plateau, where you will be greeted by long vistas of serrated splendor. Descending from the heights, you will pass through the time-worn, ancient hamlet Le Rachas, where nothing ever happens except suspended animation.

After skirting the limpid azure-blue lake formed by the damming of the Chassezac River, you will find yourself ambling along an abandoned "ghost road." Formerly D906, this stretch of crumbling concrete was recently replaced by a more direct but less scenic motor route to Villefort. Now primarily a pedestrian route, the old road (something like America's Route 66 where some of the old road signs still exist) traces the course of the deep and expansive Gorge (canyon) de Chassezac where you can often see the fast-flowing river at the bottom. Remarkable views everywhere are punctuated by astonishing world-class vistas at several points.

Emerging from the ghost road you will ramble rhapsodically into La Garde Guérin, a living medieval town. Here a lonely eleventh-century *donjon*, encircled by deteriorating stone fortifications, abuts a tiny but captivating assemblage of stone houses also surrounded by a coarse, rocky perimeter. Before the final approach to Villefort relax in the charming courtyard restaurant of the local hotel—no cars, no noise, no stress.

Tear yourself from the serene ambience of La Garde Guérin, and amble down la voie Regordaine, a Roman road that was still used during medieval times (and up to the eighteenth century) for pilgrimage and transhumance. Watch for the granite slabs laboriously placed during the Middle Ages to aid wagons in their arduous journeys along this often rain-saturated ridge of rugged terrain.

Descending steeply from la voie Regordaine, you will trace the shore of beautiful Lac de Villefort, where mutable but often benign waters delight water-sport devotees of all kinds. Veering from the lake shore, you will follow D906 into the attractively situated, green-valley town of Villefort, which serves as an excellent overnight sojourn. You may be inclined to stay more than a single evening, particularly if you enjoy outdoor sports. This magnificent area is ideal for all sorts of water sports, horseback riding, hiking, and rock climbing. During the winter, Villefort caters to downhill and cross-country skiers. There are ample accommodations and dining opportunities in this fine outdoorsperson's town.

Optional Maps/topo-guides: Série Bleu 2739 est/2738 est; GR 7 (reference #704) Sur la Ligne de Partage des Eaux: Pilat/Aigoual

Time/Distance: 3 hours 40 minutes/9.5 miles (15.2 kilometers)

Difficulties: One ten-minute climb; one long, rocky descent—wear boots

Toilet Facilities: None, but some privacy

Refreshments: None between towns

Getting There: Two trains run daily, both in the afternoon, from Villefort to the train station at Prévenchères. If you wish to leave earlier call a taxi at 66 46 80 47 or 66 46 80 09. The tourist office can also help you locate a driver.

Trail Notes

___ 1a. From the train station at Prévenchères turn left along the asphalt road that leads to D906.

___ 1b. About a minute or two later you will see a wide grassy trail to your right leading upward (the only trail). Continue to walk along this trail as it winds around until it reaches the top of the hill.

___ 1c. When you reach the top of the hill, turn right along a wide intersecting grassy trail that parallels a wire fence (the only trail), where you will begin to see waymarks.

___ 2. At Le Rachas stay on the narrow asphalt road that winds through the hamlet.

___ 3. When you reach D906, turn left and follow the road.

___ 4. After crossing a bridge you will come to an intersection with another asphalt road that used to be D906 until the present, straighter D906 was built a few years ago. Turn left here; you will follow this road for about four miles (do not go off onto any of the side roads and IGNORE ANY WAYMARKS THAT YOU MAY SEE).

___ 5. Just before you reach the new D906, go left at a trail that is marked and takes you to La Garde Guérin.

___ 6. After visiting La Garde Guérin, walk back to D906, cross the road, and go left along a grassy trail that you cannot miss and that is marked.

___ 7a. After descending for some time on the voie Regordaine, you will reach a road; cross the road, go slightly to your right and continue to descend on the trail.

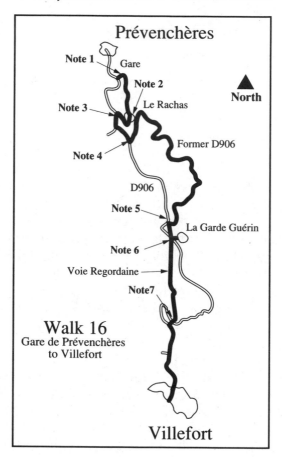

Prévenchères

Note 1 — Gare

Note 2

Le Rachas

Note 3

North

Former D906

Note 4

D906

Note 5

La Garde Guérin

Note 6

Voie Regordaine

Note7

Walk 16
Gare de Prévenchères
to Villefort

Villefort

___ 7b. When you reach the road again, go left and follow the road (D906) into town (usually there is a path or wide shoulder on one side or the other of the road).

Suggestions for More Walking

You can extend this walk an extra 5.5 miles by taking the train to the next stop, La Bastide-Puylaurent. The only way of shortening it (by about 1.5 miles) is to stay at the Hôtel du Lac, calling a taxi to pick you up at the hotel, and ending your walk at the hotel, which is not far from the point where you rejoin the road. There are numerous other walking opportunities in the park and the tourist office can help you with further suggestions.

Walk 17: Provence: Avignon

Walk: Roquemaure to Villeneuve-les-Avignon (Avignon)

140 mins.
7 miles (11.2 km)

General Description

Roquemaure, an attractive city built around a number of comely and intimate squares, luxuriates in tree-lined shaded comfort. There is nothing special to see here, but you will want to linger in this pristine town unmarred (you and the town) by roving gangs of tourists. Stop for a drink or a meal; or, perhaps, spend the night in estimable tranquility.

Leaving the leafy languor of Roquemaure, you will enter an arid, brilliantly-illuminated world that offers a wonderful sequence of astonishing vistas. Traverse bountiful vineyards while contemplating tonight's fine wine; tunnel through densely forested areas that offer welcome respite from intense solar activity; and trek high on a quiet plateau with awesome views of the mountains and valley forming today's dramatic backdrop.

Traversing this most celebrated Rhône Valley landscape, you will be surprised and delighted by an oddly placed sculpture that appears to have been constructed by Jean Arp. However, there is no signature and no indication as to why someone would have gone to such lengths to place a work of art in the middle of nowhere; perhaps, stunned by the sun, I was hallucinating. Write me if you see this thing.

Your approach to Villeneuve-les-Avignon will be enhanced by unique views of the mighty, fourteenth-century Fort St-André, which is one of the finest fortifications extant from the Middle Ages.

Within the fortifications are a Benedictine abbey and a twelfth-century chapel. Wall-climbers will revel in the magnificent views of Avignon, the Rhône River Valley, and distant Mont Ventoux.

Marching through an historic gate, you will enter Villeneuve-les-Avignon, which resides anonymously, but not bereft of worthy sights, across the Rhône from its celebrated neighbor Avignon. In addition to remarkable Fort St-André, you will also want to tour Chartreuse (charter house) du Val de Bénédiction, which was established by the Pope during the fourteenth century. A quick tour will include the well preserved church, two cloisters, and a medieval cemetery. Die-hard museum-goers will want to visit the municipal museum, which houses many artifacts from Fort St-André's abbey and la Chartreuse du Val de Bénédiction.

Street life and general sophistication pale in comparison to Avignon, but Villeneuve is not a tourist mecca or even a tourist Peoria. However, a quick stroll through this gritty, sundrenched jumble of stone structures will form a conspicuous contradistinction to the conspicuous consumption that awaits across the river.

Avignon, walled city of abducted popes (a fourteenth-century pope was dragged here by a tax-weary French king), is a wonderful base for walking under the warm provençal sun. Famous for its Palace of the Popes and collapsed bridge Pont St-Bénézet ("Pont d'Avignon" of children's song fame), Avignon is now a lively center for drama and the arts. During the summer this youthful medieval city blossoms with all types of entertainment and night life. City squares and narrow cobblestone streets are filled with musicians, mimes, acrobats, jugglers, and medieval processions. There is no finer city strolling than in this most elegant of meridianal municipalities. However, when you tire of walls and revelers, exit a gate and step into the brilliantly illuminated provençal back country.

Optional Maps/topo-guides: Série Bleu 3042 ouest; GR 42 (reference #411) Corniches Rive Droite du Rhône: Aux Portes des Cévennes

Time/Distance: 2 hours 20 minutes/7 miles (11.2 kilometers)

Difficulties: One eight-minute climb just beyond Truel

Toilet Facilities: None between cities, but much privacy

Refreshments: None between cities

Getting There: Buses (les Rapides Sud-Est, tel. 90 82 48 50; information also available at the tourist office) depart for Roquemaure (line Bagnoles-sur-Cèze) just east of the Avignon train station 2–3 times per day during the summer but less frequently during the rest of the year. If you have a car, it is best to park it and take the bus from the bus stop across the river at Villeneuve-les-Avignon directly beneath the enormous Fort St-André castle. This will save you approximately 30 to 40 minutes of road walking back to Avignon. On the other hand, by walking back to Avignon, you will enjoy some excellent views of the city.

Trail Notes

__ 1a. From the bus stop at Roquemaure, cross the street and turn right where you see the signs leading to the Mairie and the Office du Tourisme (not where signs indicate la Poste or Centre Médico-Social).

__ 1b. Within a short block you will enter a city square where the tourist office is located (place de la Mairie), turn left at the first street and continue straight ahead on rue de l'Egalité where you will see a waymark.

__ 1c. After walking a block down rue de l'Egalité, turn left on a street that is not named and then right at the first intersecting street, rue du Portalet (which becomes rue du Pavillon), which you will follow out of town

__ 2. Just beyond Roquemaure, you will pass under a railway bridge. Look to your left for the correct path. It is well marked but abrupt.

__ 3. At Truel, you will dead end at an asphalt road. Go left.

__ 4. Just beyond Truel, watch for the right turn, which is marked,

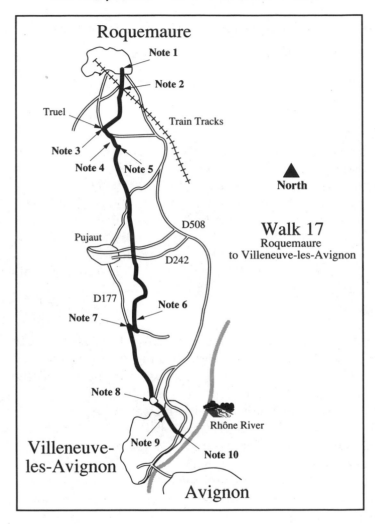

Roquemaure

Note 1

Note 2

Truel

Train Tracks

Note 3

Note 4   Note 5

▲
North

D508

Pujaut

Walk 17
Roquemaure
to Villeneuve-les-Avignon

D242

D177

Note 6

Note 7

Note 8

Rhône River

Villeneuve-
les-Avignon

Note 9

Note 10

Avignon

that goes up a narrow gravel path rather than continuing straight on the asphalt road. You will follow this path to the hill top as it narrows and becomes more difficult to distinguish. (Do not worry about the exact route to the top of the hill.)

___ 5. When you get to the top of the hill, turn right on the only path, which is narrow and rocky; you will soon see a waymark.

___ 6. Just before you reach D177 you will come to a place where you are confronted by four parallel paths. The third from your left is marked, but they all end up in the exact same place so it doesn't make any difference which one you choose to take. When they meet again, just continue straight ahead.

___ 7. When you reach D177, turn left (you will know this road since it is bearing vehicular traffic; also there is a yield sign and a sign pointing in the direction you came from: "Cimetière des Perrières")

___ 8. When you reach the newly built traffic circle, take the direction "Avignon/centre ville"; there is a waymark.

___ 9. When you enter Villeneuve-les-Avignon follow the "centre historique" signs.

___ 10. When you come to D980 (the road the bus took to Roquemaure) turn left if you parked your car near Fort St-André or if you wish to return to the bus stop to take a local bus back to Avignon. Turn right if you wish to walk the extra thirty to forty minutes back to Avignon (there are great views of the city as you cross the bridge).

Suggestions for More Walking

There is no way of shortening this walk, but it can be extended by about four miles by taking the bus to St-Genies-de-Comolas and then walking along D101 to St-Laurent-les-Arbres, where you can join the trail. For another attractive hike through the provençal landscape, try the six-mile walk from Montfrin to Beaucaire (just southwest of Avignon), which has regular bus service and is described in the abovementioned topo-guide.

Walk 18: Provence: Villages

Walk: Les Baux-de-Provence to St-Rémy-de-Provence

110 mins.
5 miles (8 km)

General Description

Les Baux-de-Provence rises directly out of a rocky promontory that surveys the appropriately named boulder-burdened and burning Val d'Enfer (Hell's Valley). Exult in the crumbling, surreal atmosphere of the Cité Mort (formerly the citadel, now called the dead city, which unfortunately has many live tourists—none of whom you will see on the trail) where it is said that lust for blood (or perhaps just simple lust) led the masters of this rock to commit many heinous and reprehensible deeds. The lords of Baux were a tough enough gang to gain control over dozens of towns and villages. Typical of local leadership, Raymond de Turenne made a business of kidnapping and ransom. Of course not everyone wanted to see their "loved ones" returned, and fun-loving Raymond enjoyed watching these refuseniks jump (perhaps over the despair of rejection but presumably under duress) off castle walls. Today, Les Baux has a quiet charm that is hard to find in most European towns—there are no cars. Amble safely along narrow corridors examining the well-preserved Renaissance homes; frequent art galleries; tour the twelfth-century church of St-Vincent; and repose at one of the cafés that hang precipitously from the cliffs offering for a not-too-steep price a priceless view of the vertiginous countryside.

You will depart from Les Baux and into Van Gogh-immortalized landscape along a narrow, rocky trail. Look over your shoulder; the citadel takes a menacing posture. Watch for jumpers. As you descend from the plateau, the land becomes forested and the soon-encountered banks of the man-made Lac de Saint-Rémy offer cool refuge from the midday sun. After tearing yourself from this forested shelter, you will quickly arrive at the Roman town of Glanum, which harbors a triumphal arch and the remains of temples, baths, and homes. Glanum's *pièce de résistance*, the final resting place of the Emperor Augustus's two grandsons, is one of the best preserved Roman mausoleums anywhere. Just beyond Glanum, along the road called allée Saint-Paul, lies the twelfth-century Monastère Saint-Paul de Mausole, where the deeply-disturbed Vincent Van Gogh was treated in 1889 and 1890. Feeling demented? Stop for a long rest.

After exploring the ruins, complete the walk to Saint-Rémy-de-Provence, birthplace of the oracle Nostradamus. Stroll comfortably along tree-lined avenues in this most shady and delightful provençal town; linger at a café—Van Gogh did; and visit the Sade House's collection of antiquities (sorry, no connection to the Marquis and no interesting restraining devices).

Optional Maps/topo-guides: Série Bleu 3042 ouest; GR 6 (reference #601) M*gne* De Lure Alpilles, Sisteron—Tarascon (pp. 58–60)

Time/Distance: 1 hour 50 minutes/5 miles (8 kilometers)

Difficulties: One short climb

Toilet Facilities: None, but occasional privacy

Refreshments: Cafés and restaurants at Les Baux and Saint-Rémy-de-Provence

Getting There: Drive south from Avignon on D571, which passes through Châteaurenard to Saint-Rémy-de-Provence. From Saint-Rémy take the bus to Les Baux (currently two per day; tel. Rapides du Sud-Est 90 82 51 75) where you will begin the walk. Alternatively you may wish to take a taxi. Via public transportation from Avignon, take the bus (same bus as mentioned above) to Les Baux; walk to Saint-Rémy; and return by bus to Avignon. Currently you will arrive at Les Baux around 11 a.m. and return from Saint-Rémy at around 5 p.m., which will allow time for the walk and some touring at both towns.

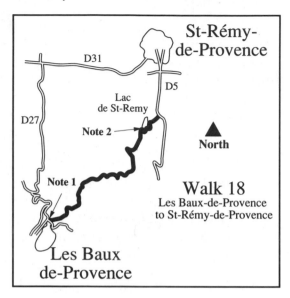

Trail Notes

__ 1. From the parking lot at the building where the bus stops, face the road, turn left, and as you walk in this direction, look to your left for a trail that goes up steeply. It is marked and easy to see.

__ 2. The trail is well marked until you reach Lac de Saint-Rémy, where you will follow the eastern bank of the lake in a northerly direction until you see a waymark, which will take you up and to the right in a very steep climb. After emerging on the other side of a steep cliff, the trail is well marked into Saint-Rémy.

Suggestions for More Walking

Although there is no way of lengthening or shortening this walk, try the longer walk from Tarascon to Les Baux (13 miles or take a cab from Tarascon to Chapelle Saint-Gabrielle and then walk the nine miles to Les Baux). Information is in the topo-guide mentioned above. Also outlined in this topo-guide is the splendid twelve-mile walk between two of Provence's finest villages, Gordes and Fontaine-de-Vaucluse.

Walk 19: Côte d'Azur: Saint-Tropez

Walk: Plage de Pampelonne to Saint-Tropez

General Description

| 170 mins. 7.5 miles (12 km) |

Lovers of the human body will linger long at the Plage de Pampelonne where, during the summer, there are more square inches of flesh than grains of sand. When you begin to suffer from ocular fatigue, start along the littoral-hugging trail to the next dazzling beach. The trail, frequently forested, is punctuated by a variety of large and small beaches. All are topless, and some of the smaller strands are nude. Stop where you feel comfortable, swim, relax, and continue your merry march.

Saint-Tropez was named for one of Nero's Christian officials, Torpes (Tropez), who refused to abjure his faith. The results of refusing the stubborn Nero were predictable: Torpes' head and body were separated. The body, miraculously preserved, washed ashore at the site of the present city. The head is yet to be heard from. Saint-Tropez is a congenial but crowded locale to spend a couple of days. Walk, swim, burn, and lounge; it gets no finer.

Optional Maps/topo-guides: Série Bleu 3545 ouest; Littoral Varois 11 Petites Randonées (reference #017) (pp. 40–43)

Time/Distance: 2 hours 50 minutes/7.5 miles (12 kilometers)

Difficulties: Many minor ups and downs

Toilet Facilities: At some beaches along the way

Refreshments: Refreshment stands, cafés, or restaurants at larger beaches

Getting There: From the *gare routière* (bus station), next to the tourist office at Saint-Tropez, take the bus to Plage de Pampelonne. Schedules are posted and also available at the tourist office. Currently, one bus leaves about 11 a.m. and another about 3 p.m.

Trail Notes

NOTE: The waymarks for this trail will be yellow.

___ 1. At the Plage de Pampelonne, turn left and walk along the beach towards Saint-Tropez. Along the beaches, you will not see any waymarks.

___ 2. You will cross the Plage de Pampelonne and the Plage de Tahiti. On both beaches, which interconnect, you will see partitions, which mark private sectors. You are welcome to walk around them in continuing your walk.

___ 3. The trail is generally well-marked; you should have no difficulties in returning to Saint-Tropez.

Suggestions for More Walking

The two coastal walks that I have selected are the most easily accessible via public transportation. However, if you will be spending extra time on the Côte d'Azur, there are nine other walks described in the *Littoral Varois* topo-guide. Most of these can be completed with the aid of public transportation; the two island walks can be segmented into a variety of lengths by returning to the starting point on secondary roads. GR 5–52 in the mountains above Nice offers good continuous walking with adequate lodging. A tranquil two-day escape from the crowds could be effected by walking from Sainte-Claire to Aspremont, spending the night at one of the two local hotels (St-Jean 93 08 00 66; Aspremont 93 08 00 05) and walking the three hours into Nice the next morning.

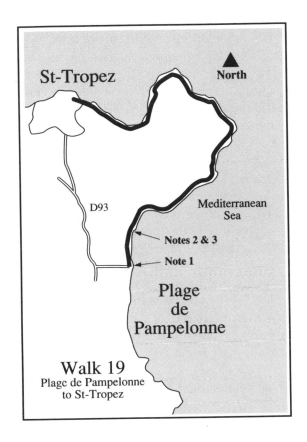

St-Tropez

▲
North

D93

Mediterranean
Sea

Notes 2 & 3

Note 1

Plage
de
Pampelonne

Walk 19
Plage de Pampelonne
to St-Tropez

Walk 20: Côte d'Azur: The French Riviera

Walk: **Les Sirènes to Saint-Aygulf**

General Description

This narrow strip of land, bordered
on one side by the deep-blue waters

150 mins.
5.6 miles (9 km)

of the Mediterranean and enclosed on the other side by the rocky slopes of the Prochaine Alps, harbors more tourists than Mecca on a holy day. This is an area of unmatched beauty, but if you go in July or August, stress and too-numerous DROPS will be your constant companions. All public services—hotels, restaurants, stores, and transportation—are overburdened during this period. After a short stay you may long for the tranquility of more remote regions. If you can go only during the peak season, be certain to reserve time for this anxiety-reducing walk, which will aid in your quest to jettison the crowds.

Les Sirènes is an appropriately named bus stop only moments from the Mediterranean Sea where your coastal walk begins. In Homer's *Odyssey*, the lure of the Sirens' song could not be resisted, just as today, the lure of the Mediterranean and its incomparable splendor proves irresistible. Alternating between sandy beach and rugged, rocky pathways, today's trail will take you through the crowds of bronzed and lobster-red beach potatoes and onto secluded, seldom visited coastal enclaves. Your walk will end at the pleasant resort of Saint-Aygulf, which has a broad, sandy but too popular beach.

Optional Maps/topo guides: Série Bleu 3544 est/3545 ouest; Littoral Varois 11 Petites Randonnées (reference #017) (pp. 44–47)

Time/Distance: 2 hours 30 minutes/5.6 miles (9 kilometers)

Difficulties: Many minor ups and downs

Toilet Facilities: Only at Saint-Aygulf

Refreshments: Cafés and restaurants at Saint-Aygulf

Getting There: Drive to Saint-Aygulf, which is between Saint-Tropez and Saint-Raphaël on N98. There is a small covered bus stop in the town center called "Saint-Aygulf la Poste." Parking is nearby. From here you will take the bus, in the direction of Saint-Tropez, to the stop called "Les Sirènes." Be certain the driver remembers

that you wish to get off at this stop, and be vigilant in watching for it. The schedule for the frequent SODETRAV buses should be posted at all bus stops, or you can pick one up at the tourist office at Saint-Tropez or Saint-Maxime. They are also available at the SODETRAV office in Saint-Raphaël (94 95 24 82)

Trail Notes

NOTE: The waymarks for this trail will be yellow.

___ 1. From the bus stop "Les Sirènes," walk back on the road in the direction of Saint-Aygulf. Look to your right; about three minutes from the bus stop, you will see a sign "Accès Sentier Littoral." Descend to the coast here and go left.

___ 2. The trail is fairly well marked, and follows the coast throughout except for the two times when you must walk along N98 for short distances that are both well marked.

___ 3. Your walk along the coast ends at a place called the "Calanque de Louvans," which is marked by a sign. Turn left up a

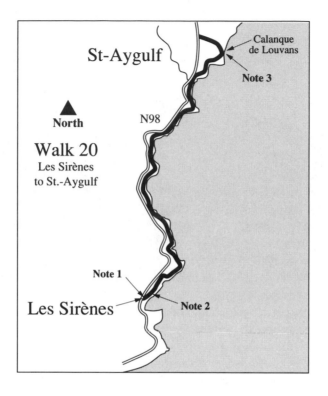

street where you will see a hotel called "La Palangrotte." Walk up to N98, and turn right. The bus stop will appear.

Suggestions for More Walking

See Walk 19's suggestions.

Walk 21: The Alps: Chamonix/ Mont-Blanc

Walk: Argentière to Chamonix

General Description

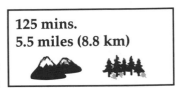

125 mins.
5.5 miles (8.8 km)

Argentière is a smaller version of its more ancient rival, Chamonix, but it also serves as an excellent base for winter and summer alpine frolicking. Take a quick tour of the town, a jumble of shops, restaurants, and chalets, or "do lunch."

Begin your walk in an enchanting, fragrant coniferous forest. The views are stunning throughout as you kick your way through the pine cones under the benign but awesome presence of Europe's highest mountain, Mont-Blanc. From time to time tear your eyes from the high-mountain panorama and commune with the serenity of the picturesque valley floor: stroll out of the forest and through an occasional meadow illuminated with an effusion of wild flowers; ford numerous but shallow mountain streams as they race fluidly down steep mountainsides (no danger beyond wet feet); and follow that quicksilver sliver of outdoor air conditioning, the Arve River, which pumps cool air on sweltering summer days to dusty trails. The valley way to Chamonix is a visual banquet rivalled by few walks anywhere.

Even crowded with international mountain climbers, local drunks, and various other DROPS, Chamonix is difficult to dislike. A valley town, Chamonix is surrounded by the snow-capped verticality of some of the highest peaks in Europe, including imposing Mont-Blanc, Europe's tallest peak. Magnificent mountain vistas combined with rapidly fluctuating, Impressionistic atmospheric effects result in a serrated, entertaining tapestry enjoyed from any café or other vantage point in this venerable mountain community. In spite of its popularity, Chamonix offers large numbers of

easily-found, reasonably-priced accommodations. However, if you enjoy sleeping at night, find a room where there is little pedestrian traffic; Bacchus-worshipping revellers party long into the night. If you plan to sojourn for a week or more, the tourist office can help you find a studio apartment or chalet. (When renting a studio, be certain to specify that you desire a location away from courtyards where clamorous youths congregate.) Do not miss this most alpine of alpine villages.

Optional Maps/topo-guides: Série Bleu Top 25 3630 OT Chamonix Massif du Mont Blanc; also a variety of locally produced booklets and maps available at the tourist office and bookstores

Time/Distance: 2 hours 5 minutes/5.5 miles (8.8 kilometers)

Difficulties: One eight-minute climb near Les Tines, and numerous minor ups and downs

Toilet Facilities: None between towns, some privacy

Refreshments: None between towns

Getting There: From the train station at Chamonix, take one of the frequent daily trains to Argentière. The schedule is posted at the station where you can pick up a copy to study. Frequent buses also run to Argentière; the bus schedule is also posted in front of the train station.

Trail Notes

___ 1a. When you emerge from the train, walk to the only road in sight (N506) and turn left.

___ 1b. Turn right along the path (chemin de la Corne à Bouc) just before you reach the railway bridge and walk parallel to the tracks. You will see a sign indicating "Petit Balcon Sud." From this point, the trail is well marked and easy to follow. Just follow the signs indicating "Petit Balcon Sud."

___ 2. You will come to an unmarked fork just beneath a massive set of cable car wires. Follow the direction marked by the sign indicating "La Flegère/La Floria." You will soon see a sign indicating "Petit Balcon Sud." Do not go down and to your left.

___ 3a. When you reach an asphalt road, you are in Chamonix. Just continue to descend.

___ 3b. When you arrive at a small traffic circle, go left and continue to descend on rue Mummery.

___ 3c. Turn right at the dead end onto rue Joseph Vallot, which takes you to the town center

Suggestions for More Walking

Many books describe trails in the vicinity of Chamonix. I recommend *Mont-Blanc Trails Guide and Map 162: Summer Walks and Hikes* which has been translated into English and includes the official tourist office twenty-franc map "Chamonix Carte des Sentiers d'Eté." You could probably get by with the map alone, but the book has some helpful notes on how to get to starting points and some

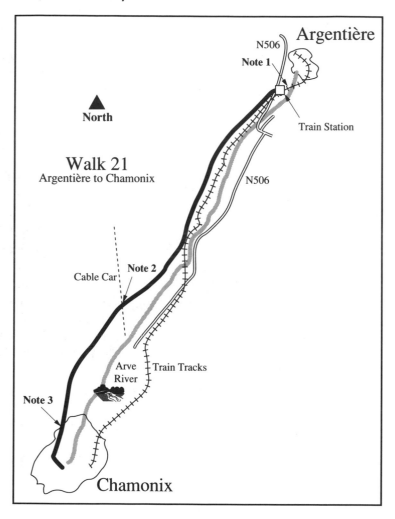

notes on the trails themselves. It also contains information, including telephone numbers, about the numerous refuges that are located along the trails and that offer attractive but usually rustic food and lodging.

You can easily plan day hikes that will coincide with buses and trains or simply take linear walks back and forth. The heavillytreed lake and riverside walk along the valley floor from Chamonix to Les Houches is tranquil and not too crowded. Any of the higher walks reached by cable cars will offer striking views of the mountains and valley below, but you will not be alone.

Backpackers can march breathlessly along one of the most famous walks in the world, the Tour Mont-Blanc, which passes through France, Italy, and Switzerland. The guide for this busy trail, which is conveniently punctuated by mountain refuges, is available in English at several local bookstores and also in Paris.

Walk 22: Cluny: The Great Abbey

Walk: **Lournand to Cluny**

General Description

60 mins.
3 miles (48 km)

Walking into Lournand, you will pass a series of very attractive homes, often constructed with beautiful golden hued stones that glisten when struck by rays of the sun. Contentedly grazing crows loiter about the homes, and vast fields of golden sunflowers, beautiful enough to stop Van Gogh in his tracks, easel and all, cascade delicately from luminous hilltops. Observing this bucolic scene from high above is a lonely, hill-top church perched at a high point in Lournand.

Athough this portion of the trail skirts the tiny hamlet, the walk into Lournand, where the structures of everyday life have changed little over the centuries, is worth the few extra minutes. Here, where commerce is unknown, freedom-loving chickens roam amiably about narrow corridors; people are seldom seen; and the appellation "ghost town" is almost appropriate.

Beyond Lournand, you will walk high along a ridge with excellent vistas of farmlands, vineyards, and forests in this beautiful hill country. You will also see and hear the streamlined TGV trains

(TGV=*train-grande-vitesse*=high-speed train) in the distance going at near-light speed. Approaching Cluny, you will be regaled by outstanding views (accessible only to pedestrians) of the town and the abbey.

The entry into Cluny, along narrow, medieval-looking streets with some homes dating back to the twelfth century, is to be savored, as is the small-town ambience that Cluny retains in spite of an omnipresent multitude of abbey groupies. Shopkeepers greet regulars and strangers alike with a warmth encountered in few other tourist centers; miniscule town squares and narrow, obscure alleyways serve as lively social centers; and an immense calm enshrouds the evening as day trippers hastily retreat along dark, serpentine roads.

During the Middle Ages, the abbey at Cluny loomed over an ecclesiastical empire that stretched across Europe and held spiritual sway over much of the continent's religious activity. The abbey was founded in 910 in order to purify increasing clerical corruption. Under a strict regime, the Cluniac monks' mission was a temporary success but a long-term failure. The old story of wealth and power corrupting may not have been as old back then but it was just as true. The Cluniac monks eventually became a wealthy cabal of sybaritic power brokers whose influence slowly waned during the centuries until it disappeared in an anti-clerical tide of sentiment during the French Revolution. The church, the largest in Christendom until the construction of Saint Peter's in Rome, was quickly dismantled by stone-hungry masons. All that remains is one of the transepts, but the enormity of this awesome ruin is amazing and evocative of the massiveness of the once complete structure. The official tour informs well, but idle about on your own for a while reconstructing and visualizing the past of this remarkable site.

Optional Maps/topo-guides: Série Bleue 2927 est; although this trail is marked with the official red and white waymarks, no topo-

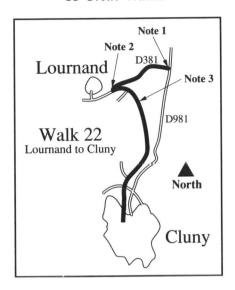

guide has been published

Time/Distance: One hour/3 miles (4.8 kilometers)

Difficulties: A gentle but long climb up to Lournand

Toilet Facilities: None

Refreshments: None

Getting There: Several buses (les Cars du Val de Saône, tel. 85 81 10 92 or 85 38 16 09) per day leave Cluny from the bus stop at the rue Porte de Paris. Schedules and information are available at the tourist office.

Trail Notes

___ 1a. The bus will let you off on D981; it is too big to go up into the town of Lournand itself.

___ 1b. Walk back in the direction of Cluny; you will almost immediately see a sign indicating "Lournand 2 kilomètres."

___ 1c. Take this narrow asphalt road in the direction of Lournand.

___ 2. Just before you enter the town you will see a sign indicating "Lournand." At this point, you will notice that a road coming down from your left intersects with the road that you are on. Turn left, and follow this road upward. (You will begin to see waymarks at this point.)

___ 3. When you come to a fork, go right; it is marked. From this point the trail is well marked and easy to follow into Cluny.

Suggestions for More Walking

This walk cannot be altered using public transportation, but for a slightly longer (5 miles), southern approach to Cluny take the one morning bus per day to St-Cécile, where you can join the trail. This involves crossing N79 (the main road that the bus traverses) and turning left at the narrow asphalt road that runs briefly parallel. Purchase the Série Bleu 2928 est map, which clearly shows the route.

Walk 23: Jura: France's Switzerland

Walk: Château Trail: Passenans to Domblans

90 mins.
4.5 miles (7.2 km)

General Description

This is a wonderfully eventful journey through an enchanted countryside, starting at the remote (about as remote as possible for a functioning station—it is surprising to find someone still living and working here) but still inhabited train station at Passenans. A quick, scenic jaunt from the station will land you dead center in downtown Passenans, an attractive weather-beaten town constructed from sparkling golden hued stone. Stop for refreshments or, better yet, imbibe from the beautiful fountain where the cool, highly drinkable spring water refreshes even the most parched of throats.

Passing from Passenans, you will traverse bountiful vineyards and stroll adjacent to encroaching forests on your way to the remarkable *château* and church of Frontenay. The *château* is a wonderfully restored medieval fortress and the fabulous, still-attended fourteenth-century church constitutes a perfect counterpoint. The synergy of this ensemble, enshrouded deep in a protective forest and seldom visited because of its remoteness, results in an unparalleled visual celebration. It is truly an ethereal vision and one of the most alluring sights on any trail in France. A superb cemetery and small mausoleum complete this lovely complex. The verdant, steeply descending path leading from the *château*/church into the very attractive town is the route reverent stout-legged townspeople followed to the church during the pre-automobile era.

Departing Frontenay, you will soon be in Blandans via a forested, leafy green tunnel. At the end of this verdant corridor lies the meticulously restored Château de Blandans. Constructed in the fifteenth century, this *château* is currently inhabited and not able to be visited. However, it forms a wonderful prop for fantasies about splendid isolation in this most arcadian ambience.

About twenty minutes later, you will stroll into the lovely town of Domblans and past yet another *château*. The inhabited, not-able-to-be-visited Château de Domblans, also constructed during the fifteenth century, forms an attractive finale to an unusually resplendent romp through forests, fields, towns, and *châteaux*. Relax in town while processing so many visual delights.

Optional Maps/topo-guides: Série Bleue 3226 est; GR 59 (reference #510) Des Vosges au Jura: Ballon d'Alsace à Lons-le-Saunier

Time/Distance: 1 hour 30 minutes/4.5 miles (7.2 kilometers)

Difficulties: Several climbs, some difficult

Toilet Facilities: None

Refreshments: Passenans, Domblans

Getting There: Domblans is about eight miles north of Lons-le-Saunier. Two to three trains per day link Domblans with Passenans. The schedule is posted at the station and it is always possible to get scheduling information at any train station in France. Buses also link the two cities and the bus stop with a posted schedule at Domblans is near the train station.

Trail Notes

NOTE: You will be following yellow waymarks. Ignore the yellow and green and red and white waymarks.

___ 1a. When you depart from the train, walk through or around the Passenans train station and turn right at the road that leads to the train station.

___ 1b. Follow the road downhill. You will see a sign at the first road that indicates "Passenans 1.3 kilomètres." Turn right here and follow the asphalt road (D43) into town.

___ 2. When you get to the center of town, turn right on D57 where you see the large traffic sign indicating "Frontenay 1.5 kilomètres."

___ 3. As you walk out of Passenans on D57, you will see a bus shelter (not the one in the center of town). Look to your left: just before you see the bus shelter you will see the hotel/restaurant and a yellow waymark. Turn left here and continue to follow the yellow waymarks. You will pass by the hotel and climb into vineyards.

___ 4. When you see the Château de Frontenay perched high on its hill top continue to walk directly towards it along a barbed wire fence. You will not see a waymark until you are almost at the *château*.

___ 5. As you walk out of Frontenay on a grassy path, you will reach an asphalt road, which you will follow in the same direction.

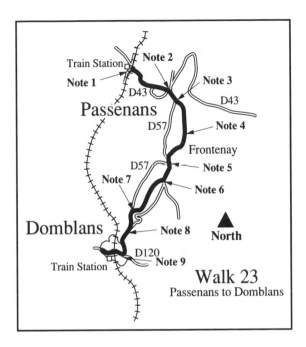

Walk 23
Passenans to Domblans

___ 6. After reaching the asphalt road mentioned above, you will soon reach a point where the road bifurcates. Just before you reach the bifurcation, look for a trail that leads to the right and up into the forest. It is not marked at this juncture (although you will see other waymarks), but you will see the waymarks in the forest. (The road that goes directly ahead also goes to Blandans but is less scenic.)

___ 7. Just before you leave the forest, there is a path to the left that is well marked but easy to miss. If you leave the forest and reach a road, go back and look for the turn.

___ 8. The trail does not go directly into Domblans. Just before you reach Domblans the trail makes a sharp right turn; directly ahead you will see a large traffic sign indicating "Domblans" on a bridge. Follow this road into town.

___ 9. When you get to D120, a heavily trafficked road, go right and you will soon see the train station to your left.

Suggestions for More Walking

Excellent walking opportunities that correspond with reliable public transportation abound in this area. The aerobic nine miles between the resort Salins-les-Bains and postcard pretty Arbois is most gratifying, as is the eight miles from Arbois to petite Poligny—a walk that includes a surprise Roman sanctuary in a remote, deeply wooded site. The ten miles between Poligny and Passens completes the link from Salins-les-Bains to the walk described above. Consult Série Bleu maps 3225 ouest, 3225 est, and 3226 est. All of these walks are also detailed and mapped in the above-mentioned topo-guide.

Walk 24: Vezelay: The Great Pilgrimage Basilica

Walk: Asquins to Vézelay

General Description

**40 mins.
2 miles (3.2 km)**

Asquins, a sleepy town ensconced along the banks of the Cure River, basks in the nearby glory of Vézelay. This walk-through community, consisting of a motley assortment of houses, a small hotel/restaurant, butcher, baker, candlestick maker, etc., may cause you to pause if only for its winsome locale and riparian remoteness. If not, climb quickly out of Asquins and into the congenial rusticity of the surrounding landscape; your destination, the beautiful basilica at Vézelay, is in view. Approaching Vézelay on a rocky track, like the medieval pilgrims before you, will have a sense of awe as you near the venerable majesty of the basilica and spy it from an angle not allowed to vehicular traffic. On the final, breathtaking (in more ways than one) approach to Vézelay, you will pass the Cordelle Chapelle, which was constructed in the twelfth

century and served as a final prayer stop before arrival into the city. Entering the city through ancient walls, you will pass beneath the Porte Ste-Croix, gateway to multitudes of pilgrims over a millennia.

The twelfth-century Basilique de la Madeleine, where the remains of the recently-rehabilitated Mary Magdalen supposedly lie, is the crown jewel of this superb hill-top town. This romanesque gem merits a detailed exploration: tours are offered on a daily basis, and local guide books are ubiquitous. For astonishing views of the surrounding countryside climb the basilica's Tour St-Michel. As you descend from the basilica to the town center, browse in fine art galleries or buy some of the fine burgundy wine from local vineyards. The merchants are often housed in centuries-old structures; examine the buildings carefully.

Like Le-Puy-en-Velay, Vézelay served as a starting point for the pilgrimage to Santiago de Compostela. If you are in the mood for a long walk, stroll out of a gate and hike along the pilgrimage

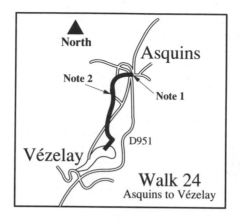

trail until, several months later, you arrive at Santiago in the north-west corner of Spain. A romantic idea; but you may well see some-one in town sporting a backpack beginning such a journey.

Optional Maps/topo-guides: Série Bleue 2722 ouest: GR 13–131 (reference #125) Des Côteaux de l'Yonne au Morvan par la Vallée de la Cure: Auxerre-Vézelay-Autun. (Although this is not part of GR 13–131, the route of this *petite randonée* is indicated on the map.)

Time/Distance: 40 minutes/2 miles (3.2 kilometers)

Difficulties: A fifteen-minute climb into Vézelay

Toilet Facilities: None between towns, but some privacy

Refreshments: None between towns

Getting There: Two buses per day (one morning and one after-noon except weekends when there is only a morning bus) run between Vézelay and the train station at Sermizelles. Asquins, not far from Vézelay, is the first stop on this route. Schedules are available at the Vézelay tourist office, or call Cars de la Madeleine at 86 33 35 95. The bus departs from the lower part of the village where the parking lots are located. Wait at the large maroon sign with white letters that indicates "Touristes Visitez Vézelay à Pied."

Trail Notes

NOTE: You will follow single red waymarks.

___ 1a. The bus will drop you at a covered shelter next to a telephone booth at Asquins. Walk back in the direction of Vézelay to the place sous l'Orme where the hotel is located.

___ 1b. At the place sous l'Orme there is a fork in the road. Go right and upwards. (Do not go down the road that runs parallel to the road that the bus came down.)

___ 1c. You will almost immediately come to a second bifurcation, where you will take the road to the left, rue de la Chèvrerie.

___ 2. At the top of rue de la Chèvrerie you will come to a dead end: go left on rue de la Bouillere; just ahead you will see a single red waymark. From this point, the trail is well marked and easy to follow.

Suggestions for More Walking

The walk from Pierre-Perthuis to Vézelay (four miles) is quite attractive and offers the option of visiting the Roman ruins at Les Fontaines Salées (add 1.5 miles); however, buses only run once or twice per week to Pierre-Perthuis. It is also possible to walk the ten miles from Sermizelles to Vézelay by taking the same daily bus that stops at Asquins. This walk is magnificent. For both of these options, consult the maps and topo-guide mentioned above.

Walk 25: Water Wonderland: Vittel/Contrexéville

Walk: Contrexéville to Vittel

General Description

Contrexéville and Vittel are famous names in France and rapidly becoming well known among mineral-water cognoscenti in the United States and Britain. The cause of such robust name recognition is the wonderfully pure mineral waters that emanate from springs in both towns. However, people do not come to these resort towns for a drink of water; they come for the baths, casinos, elegant ambience, old-world charm, and impressive turn-of-the-century architecture—splendid hotels, public buildings, and ornate grounds abound. Both towns offer an insider's look into the courtly and genteel past of France's monied classes. Although no longer out of the reach of the common man, both resorts preserve a gentility of life seldom seen anywhere else.

110 mins.
5.5 miles (8.8 km)

Contrexéville, set deep in a forested valley, affords you the wonderful experience of simply being able to walk out of an elegant town and into a countryside that is to be savored. Within a few minutes, you will be coursing down rural roads and obscure pathways, arriving in short order at a most unfrequented hamlet called Outrancourt, where no unusual occurrences have been recorded in decades. Walking out of this rural obscurity, you will soon reach the top of a hill where, in the distance, you will spy an expansive, modern shopping center. Look back to Outrancourt, France's past; look ahead to sweeping commercialism, the rapidly encroaching future.

The beautiful Forêt Parc de Vittel invites the walker into a park-like atmosphere where the crown jewel, the beautiful children's zoo, houses a pair of regally wing-spanned peacocks worthy of NBC. Definitely worth a wait for a splendid display of wing span.

Rapidly expanding Vittel offers the same amenities and valley setting found at Contrexéville. Revel in remarkable views of the surrounding Vosges mountains; repose in the pure waters of local thermal springs; and enjoy the relaxed resort atmosphere. This is an excellent area to plan idle hours.

Optional Maps/topo-guides: Série Bleu 3318 ouest, 3318 est; GR 7/714 (reference #701) Ballons et Plateaux des Vosges

Time/Distance: 1 hour 50 minutes/5.5 miles (8.8 kilometers)

Difficulties: Several minor climbs

Toilet Facilities: At the park just before Vittel

Refreshments: Refreshment stand at the park

Getting There: Several daily trains run between Vittel and Contrexéville. Schedules are available at both train stations and tourist offices at both towns.

Trail Notes

NOTE: This is a good walk to purchase a corresponding detailed map, since rapid expansion of Vittel is causing the trail to become more difficult to follow.

__ 1a. From the train station at Contrexéville, turn left and walk up the only street in the only possible direction.
__ 1b. When you reach the first fork, bear left, walking parallel to the tracks. (Turn right if you wish to spend some time in town before beginning the walk.)
__ 1c. Continue straight ahead when you intersect with the tracks.
__ 1d. When you reach D164, cross it and continue straight ahead on the road marked D13 (also called rue de Verdun).
__ 2. Continuing along D13, turn right on the road marked Outrancourt (route C6, about 1.2 miles from the train station) where you will also see a sign marking the trail as GR 714.

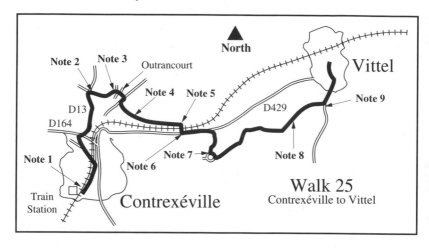

North

Note 2 Note 3 Outrancourt

Vittel

Note 4 Note 5

Note 9

D13

D429

D164

Note 1

Note 7

Note 8

Note 6

Walk 25
Contrexéville to Vittel

Train
Station

Contrexéville

___ 3. In Outrancourt make the first possible right turn, which is not marked but you will soon see a worn waymark on a concrete utility pole. (In Outrancourt the marking is not good, but your goal is to cross the bridge over the Vair River, which is easy to find.)

___ 3b. When you get to the bridge over the Vair River, cross it, go right (there is a worn waymark visible), and almost immediately make a left from the asphalt road to a dirt track which is well marked.

___ 4. As you walk down the dirt road do not go into the forest; stay parallel to the forest and the road you see to your right.

___ 5. Watch for the right turn on a small bridge over the train tracks and onto D429 which is clearly marked.

___ 6a. When you reach D429, turn left and walk along the path that parallels the road which is clearly marked.

___ 6b. Continue to look to the right (you will get there in about 10 minutes) for the point that you should cross the road and enter the forest (Forêt Parc de Vittel) on a dirt road that ascends, which is clearly marked.

___ 7. When you reach the park center (there is a small traffic circle), turn left on the trail just beyond the snack bar.

___ 8. As of the date of publication, a new road is being put through just beyond the forest. The trail is still passable at this point, and I suspect that a pedestrian overpass will be installed. However, if the trail is interrupted and no waymarks appear when you pass by, turn left and walk the short distance to D429 where you will turn right and walk into Vittel.

___ 9a. When you come to D68, you will see a sign indicating "Centre Ville"; turn left here and walk into town.

___ 9b. When you reach the first intersecting street, turn left and walk towards the highly-visible church which is in the town center.

Suggestions for More Walking

Although there is no possibility of extending or shortening this walk by using public transportation, this area is endowed with vast and numerous forests. Armed with the Série Bleu maps mentioned above, it should be easy to find your way to Bulgneville and back form Contrexéville via Lacs de la Folie by heading in the opposite direction from Outrancourt. For a longer walk take the train from either Vittel or Contrexéville southwest to Martigny-les-Bains. From Martigny, walk out on D21 about two miles to a juncture with GR 7, and turn left following the route of an ancient Roman road. To return to Contrexéville (about 10 miles), turn left at D164 and take a variety of easy-to-follow back roads to Contrexéville via Dombrot-le-Sec. To return to Vittel (about 12 miles), follow GR 714 when it forks with GR 7, turning left on D68 at Ligneville.

Walk 26: Alsace-Lorraine: Bar-le-Duc

Walk: Trémont-sur-Saulx to Bar-le-Duc

General Description

120 mins.
6 miles (9.6 km)

Trémont-sur-Saulx is an attractive rural community with various and sundry businesses strewn along its weatherbeaten main street. Enhancing Trémont's rusticity are fresh-flowing waters from the spring "Source de Saint-Sébastien," which result in a little Venice effect: many residents must span spring waters with bantam bridges in order to pass from home to street. Add an admirable church that was constructed between the thirteenth and the sixteenth centuries and the image of bucolic tranquility is complete. Passing, rails-to-trails, through Trémont along a former rail bed, you will be afforded enlightening views of the back yards that line the main street; a curious array of furry and feathered friends, abandoned cars, unkempt gardens, and unidentified lying objects grace your path. You are light years from the tourist version of France.

As you leave Trémont-sur-Saulx, homes give way to pastures, which soon become the dense, solar-eclipsing forest known as Bois Blandin that you traverse in its entirety. En route to the village of Veel, you will leave the forest and enter a Christina's World of rolling fields; the topography bears an eerie resemblance to Andrew Wyeth's signature painting. Watch for waifs lying mysteriously about.

Just before Bar-le-Duc, you will enter a motley but interesting collection of old and new homes known as Veel. A requisite, picturesque church and small *château* undergoing extensive rehabilitation form the nucleus of a town that is completely surrounded by and permeated with grazing land; corpulent sheep graze everywhere within and around the town. The final entry into Bar-le-Duc, through a road where large, superbly designed homes are almost concealed within densely forested lots, is a good look at how the wealthy live in France.

Bar-le-Duc, once the center of an extensive regional dukedom, languishes quietly only a couple of hours from Paris. Crowds of tourists are unknown here, and you will not go wrong by planning a night in this thoroughly delightful provincial capital. The *haute ville* (upper city) is the main historical attraction where the Gothic Eglise Saint-Etienne forms a striking centerpiece for surrounding homes dating back to the fifteen century along place Saint-Pierre. An inspection of the church's interior reveals the terrifying sixteenth-century *squellette* (skeleton) called "Le Transi," crafted by Ligier Richier and depicting the triumph of eternal life over death. Remains of the *château*, including La Porte Romane (dating back to the first century A.D.) and the esplanade, which provides excellent views of the city, also merit inspection.

Tranquilly situated along the banks of the Ornain River, the *basse ville* (lower town) harbors most of the commerce, including hotels and restaurants and provides all of the ingredients for a comfortable sojourn. Tireless tourists will want to visit the thirteenth-century Eglise Notre Dame via the fourteenth-century bridge Pont Notre Dame. Others will want to stroll aimlessly along pleasant avenues and calmly repose at the beautiful Clinique du Parc, which conceals a diminutive zoo within its verdant grounds.

Optional Maps/topo-guides: Série Bleu 3115 ouest; GR 14 (reference #106) D'Argonne en Ardenne

Time/Distance: 2 hours/6 miles (9.6 kilometers)

Difficulties: Several short climbs

Toilet Facilities: None, but much privacy

Refreshments: None

Getting There: Several buses per day go between Bar-le-Duc and Trémont-sur-Saulx (ultimate destination: Saint Dizier). Schedules

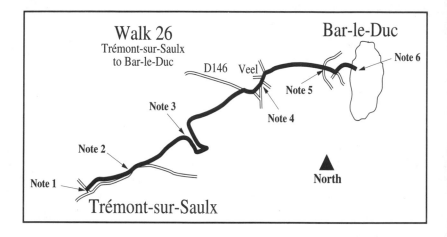

Walk 26
Trémont-sur-Saulx
to Bar-le-Duc

Bar-le-Duc

D146 Veel

Note 6

Note 5

Note 3

Note 4

Note 2

North

Note 1

Trémont-sur-Saulx

are available at the bus station (*gare routière*) or at the tourist office. They are also posted at the bus station. Buses depart from the bus station, stopping at the train station and several other locations before leaving town.

Trail Notes

___ 1a. The bus drops you off at a shelter in the center of Trémont (tell the bus driver *"centre ville"* or show him the schedule indicating *"centre"*—there is another stop on the outskirts of town.)

___ 1b. Walk back one street to rue Gustave Chenut and turn left on this street which takes you uphill.

___ 1c. A couple of minutes later, you will make a sharp right turn which takes you up and back in the direction of town. The turn is marked. Continue behind the church along the now level pathway.

___ 1d. When the road divides, take the high road.

___ 2. Just out of town you will reach D3 (the road the bus took into town) where you turn left and then quickly turn left again at a dirt trail—both turns are marked.

___ 3a. In the forest, you will reach a point where you can go left, straight ahead and up, or right. Look down the path to your right, you will see a waymark.

___ 3b. As you walk down this trail watch carefully to your left for a waymark on a tree that takes you down a narrow path to your left. The mark is there but it is easy to miss.

___ 4. At Veel, ignore the red and yellow waymarks and continue to follow the red and white waymarks.

___ 5. IMPORTANT: Just before entering Bar-le-Duc, you will come to a point where you can go left, straight ahead, or right on asphalt roads. The waymark indicates a left turn, but the trail does not go directly into town and this turn will take you away from Bar-le-Duc. Just continue straight ahead on the wide asphalt road as it winds around. Do not go down any of the narrow (single-car, driveway size) roads that intersect and you will soon be in Bar-le-Duc.

___ 6. You will enter the town on rue Montant. The first street that intersects is rue de Veel, where you will turn left and go directly to the center of town.

Suggestions for More Walking

This walk can be extended by a little more than another mile by taking the bus to the next town, Robert Espagne, where the GR 14 trail originates. You can also approach Bar-le-Duc from the north by starting at Louppy-sur-Chée (where buses run several times weekly) and walking back the 7.5 miles through an attractive countryside.

Walk 27: Champagne Country:
Château-Thierry

Walk: Chézy-sur-Marne to Château-Thierry

General Description

150 mins.
7.5 miles (12 km)

Starting at Chézy-sur-Marne, a pictur-
esque post card of a town that slumbers with nineteenth-century
grace into the very late twentieth century, you will wander quickly
across the Marne River; however, you will be no further into the
twentieth century as you enter virtual twin-town Azy-sur-Marne,
which floats photogenically in asymmetric stages along equable
river banks. Climbing high from this agreeable hamlet, you will
enter a quiet, sun-drenched world of champagne grapes—some
of the finest anywhere. As you continue to walk high above the
valley floor, your eyes will be transfixed upon the lovely waters
of the Marne River flowing languidly through rich, vine-covered
fields.

Entering Essomes from a forested pathway, you will pass directly by an elegant thirteenth-century Gothic church and then
traverse this attractive town where you can stop for food and beverage. Ascending from Essomes to a high plateau, you will be greeted
by astounding views of Château-Thierry in the distance.

Just before entering Château-Thierry, you will encounter the
American Monument, an imposing white-marble art-deco structure erected by the French in gratitude to the American soldiers
who fought and died for the liberty of France during the First
World War. From the monument's position on a high promontory, the views of Château-Thierry are unique and continue to
please as you descend to the Marne River, which you will follow
as you approach the city center. The walk along the Marne within
Château-Thierry is quite pleasant—the riverside path provides a

park-like atmosphere while pleasure craft float lazily along tranquil waters.

Historic Château-Thierry has seen the likes of major historical characters such as Charles Martel, who, in the eighth century, constructed a *château* for Thierry IV, the next-to-last Merovingian king. Also the birthplace of La Fontaine of fable fame, whose sixteenth-century house you can visit, Château-Thierry is a remarkably attractive and quiet city only a stone's throw from the bustle of Paris. The major attraction is the ruin of the thirteenth-century *château* perched high above the city. From this park-like, non-vehicular promenade, you may survey the city and lovely Marne Valley. Beneath the *château*, stroll quiet streets flanked by handsome homes; imbibe superb local champagne; and visit the attractive fifteenth-century church.

Optional Maps/topo-guides: Série Bleu 2613 ouest, 2613 est; GR 11 (reference # 104) Ile-de-France

Time/Distance: 2 hours 30 minutes/7.5 miles (12 kilometers)

Difficulties: A strenuous fifteen-minute climb out of Essomes

Toilet Facilities: None, but much privacy

Refreshments: Chézy-sur-Marne, Azy-sur-Marne, Essomes-sur-Marne.

Getting There: From the train station at Château-Thierry, take one of the several daily trains to Chézy-sur-Marne. Schedules are available at the tourist office or the train station.

Trail Notes

___ 1a. From the train station at Chézy-sur-Marne, walk to the bridge and turn right. (Your objective is the second bridge that you see in the distance, but it is not safe to walk along the tracks in order to reach it.)

___ 1b. When you reach the road D15, turn left and cross a small bridge over the Dolloin River. (You will see a road sign

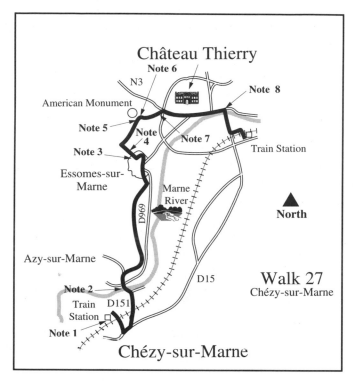

Château Thierry

Note 6

N3

American Monument

Note 5

Note 4

Note 3

Essomes-sur-Marne

Note 8

Note 7

Train Station

Marne River

North

D969

Azy-sur-Marne

Note 2

Train Station

D151

Note 1

D15

Walk 27
Chézy-sur-Marne

Chézy-sur-Marne

indicating "Château-Thierry.")

___ 1c. You will very quickly turn left on D151 (the first left after crossing the Dolloir River; another road sign indicating "Château-Thierry" is visible) and follow this road across the Marne River into Azy-sur-Marne.

___ 2. Just before entering Azy-sur-Marne, you will turn left at the end of the bridge where the trail is clearly marked into Essomes.

___ 3a. At Essomes, turn left on the street just before the Gothic church, which is rue Jeu d'Arc.

___ 3b. Watch for the right turn which is marked just after you have come to the end of a long wall.

___ 4a. As you are climbing out of Essomes, you will come to a cross where a right turn is clearly marked.

__ 4b. IMPORTANT: A short distance from the cross, where the road bifurcates, you will go left and up on a dirt trail (you are walking through an open field where there is no place to affix a waymark) where you will continue to climb past the small woods that you see, where you will begin to see waymarks again.

__ 4c. When you reach the top of the plateau, turn right along a path that is marked on a fence post.

__ 5a. Near the end of the plateau, where the road forks, turn left and into the woods.

__ 5b. Just before the American Monument, the trail splits. To the left, where the regular red and white waymarks points, is the wrong way, which will take you away from Château-Thierry. Go right where you see the deviation waymarks that take you into Château-Thierry, which you can clearly see at this point.

__ 6a. From the center of the American Monument, walk downhill to a small clearing.

__ 6b. Just to the right of the clearing there is a narrow, forested trail that you will follow straight down into town. (At first you will see only yellow waymarks, but later the red and white waymarks will begin to appear; both sets of waymarks take you into town.)

__ 7a. When you arrive in Château-Thierry, the waymarks bifurcate—yellow to the left and red and white to the right. Both sets will take you to the center of town but the yellow waymarks take a more direct approach. (The red and white waymarks take a circuitous route that is not always marked.)

__ 7b. When you reach R.N.3/avenue de Paris (assuming you have followed the yellow waymarks), go right and continue straight into town. Watch for the "centre ville" sign; you will not see any waymarks until you reach the Marne.

__ 7c. After about ten minutes, you will come to the Marne, where you can follow a riverside path to the town center.

___ 8. When you reach the bridge over the Marne, turn right and cross the river. Continue straight and watch for the signs that indicate "gare," which will take you back to the train station.

Suggestions for More Walking

Although it is not possible to shorten this walk via public transportation, there are two possibilities for extension. By continuing along on the same train to Nogent-l'Artaud, you can extend the walk by an extra four miles, and by going to the next stop at Nanteuil-sur-Marne an extra eleven miles is added for a total of almost nineteen miles. Alternatively, you can add another day's walk by traversing the seven miles between Nanteuil-sur-Marne and Nogent-l'Artaud or the four miles between Nogent-l'Artaud and Chézy-sur-Marne.

Walks 28–35: Paris: Center of the Universe

No city surpasses Paris for its walker-friendly infrastructure. Of course, there is much traffic and noise, but it is possible to wander for hours in virtually any direction and find an easy return via the Metro or buses to your starting point. Several informative books have been written about walking in Paris, but nothing has been written about the excellent walks just outside of Paris that are easily accessible through frequent public transportation. Around Paris, I have included walks that will take you to well-known tourist sites such as Versailles and Fontainebleau, but I have also included walks to places that you might not otherwise visit. All of the following walks traverse historic areas and can usually be done within the space of a few hours, including transportation. Since you will be on your feet and in motion often within Paris, most of the walks are in the short-to-medium length range. I have included only information on how to do each walk via public transportation since there is no particular need to use a car in this area. However, you can often use a car by leaving it at one train station or bus stop and walking back to retrieve it. Around Paris you must be very observant in looking for waymarks. Although the trails are usually well marked, there are many intersecting pathways which can result in confusion if you are not vigilant. Also be certain to pack adequate rain protection; it rains often around Paris and the weather can change quickly. All of these walks end at train stations from which you can return to Paris.

Walk 28: Cergy-Pontoise: Nouvelle Ville

Walk: **Cergy-Préfecture to Cergy-St-Christophe**

General Description

> 110 mins.
> 5.5 miles (8.8 km)
>
>

During the nineteen-sixties, a series of satellite cities surrounding Paris was conceived. Designed to relieve Parisian overcrowding, the *"nouvelle villes"* (new towns) were connected by rapid transit to Paris and offered a less expensive and less frenetic alternative to life in the capital. Of these towns, Cergy-Pontoise is the most attractive and extensive. Divided into several distinct villages, this vast and highly habitable agglomeration spans an area as large as Paris itself but harbors less than one-tenth the inhabitants. The community is completely self-contained: many major corporations have located here providing jobs; all types of recreation have been planned; shopping opportunities abound; and education has been provided through the university level.

The walk begins at Cergy-Préfecture, the commercial hub of the complex. From the RER train stop ascend via escalator to the quiet, car-less town above. This is how cities of the future should be constructed: everything is on a human scale here and built with people in mind. The central portion of the Préfecture is built on an extensive platform that admits no vehicular traffic (public transportation, roads, and parking exist beneath the platform) and houses a comprehensive regional shopping center, office buildings, and condominiums. Surrounding the platform are spacious tracts of green, tidy, architecturally interesting neighborhoods and commercial office towers. Everything is linked by footpaths, obviating the need for motor vehicles.

Departing Cergy-Préfecture you will follow the course of the beautiful Oise River where barges, tour boats, and pleasure cruisers float aimlessly, and fishermen phlegmatically cast slow moving flies along winsome banks. You will pass an interesting mixture of shacks, middle-class abodes, and palaces in a *mélange* of styles, from rustic to hyper-modern. The hungry will rejoice over the convenience of a couple of restaurants very nicely situated along the banks where fine food and drink may be had. Before entering Cergy-St-Christophe, you will also pass along some beautifully forested tracts while still following the course of the river.

Most of the final approach into Cergy-St-Christophe is spent along the Axe Majeur, a monumental walkway conceived by the Israeli sculptor Dani Karavan. Punctuated by terraces, gardens, esplanades, an amphitheater, sculpture, and architectural gems, the Axe Majeur offers distant views of Paris and some of the most unusual walking anywhere.

Although smaller and more residential than the Préfecture, Cergy-St-Christophe also follows the principle of separating cars and people. Along the attractive, winding streets you will find boutiques, restaurants, and attractive housing. The great clock at the place de l'Horloge just before the train station astonishes by its size, and you will be able to view it from a variety of distances as you approach the station. Take some time to wander about here; this planned community solves many of the problems engendered by explosive suburban growth elsewhere.

Optional Maps/topo-guides: Série Bleu (TOP 25) 2313 OT Forêts de

Montmorency de l'Isle-Adam et de Carnelle (the inexpensive city map available at some stores in Préfecture's shopping center is also quite helpful and shows the entire walk); PR (reference 072) A la Découverte du Val-d'Oise: 36 Promenades et Randonnées.

Time/Distance: 1 hour 50 minutes/5.5 miles (8.8 kilometers)

Difficulties: Two short climbs

Toilet Facilities: Port de Cergy; some privacy

Refreshments: Cergy-Préfecture, two restaurants along the Oise River, Port de Cergy, Cergy-St-Christophe

Getting There: From Paris, take the RER line A3 to Cergy-Préfecture. To return to Paris simply take the same line from Cergy-St-Christophe.

Trail Notes

NOTE: Follow the red and orange waymarks

___ 1. From the RER station (and where all the buses stop) turn right and walk in a south easterly direction on boulevard de l'Oise toward the Oise River (if you find yourself walking under the huge platform that supports the city you are going the wrong way; if you are going the right way, you will almost immediately pass the large U.A.P. building).

___ 2. As soon as you cross the bridge over the Oise River, turn right (it is easier to take the stairway on the left side of the bridge which, at the bottom, leads you left under the bridge instead of the very steep and narrow path on the right side of the bridge), and go south onto a very narrow asphalt road that skirts the river. You will follow this road to the next bridge.

___ 3a. When you come to the first traffic bridge (you will have already passed under a train bridge), turn right and cross the Oise River. (Waymarks will not be visible until you pass through Port-de-Cergy.)

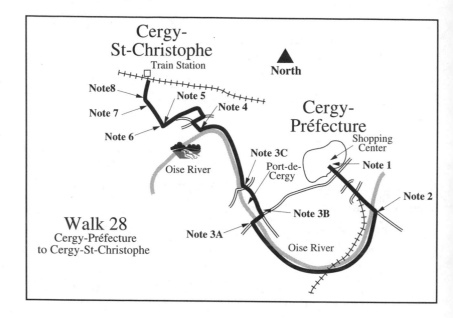

Cergy-
St-Christophe
Train Station

North

Note8
Note 5
Note 7
Note 4
Note 6

Cergy-
Préfecture

Shopping
Center

Note 3C
Port-de-
Cergy

Note 1

Oise River

Note 2

Walk 28
Cergy-Préfecture
to Cergy-St-Christophe

Note 3B

Note 3A

Oise River

___ 3b. On the other side of the bridge, take the stairway down to the narrow asphalt road that parallels the Oise River and follow the road directly into Port-de-Cergy and the place du Grand Hunier, where numerous eating and drinking opportunities await.

___ 3c. Pass through to the other side of the place du Grand Hunier, where you reach a dead end and see once again the waymarks that will take you left and down to the river where you will turn right and continue the walk (ignore the signs that limit traffic along this path; you are welcome as a hiker).

___ 4a. As you are walking along the Oise River, you will come to a large clearing where you turn right on an asphalt road called "ruelle du Port de Gency" (there is a waymark on a telephone pole).

___ 4b. When you reach the top of ruelle du Port de Gency, turn right (your first possible right) on rue Vaureal.

___ 4b. When you reach the top of ruelle du Port de Gency, turn right (your first possible right) on rue Vaureal.

___ 4c. Watch to your left for a trail that ascends called the "Sentier Laroque," which will lead you to an athletic field. (4b. and 4c. are both marked.)

___ 4d. When you reach the athletic field, take the first left along a very wide straight path that was formerly a railway bed.

___ 5. When you reach an asphalt area that offers an extensive panoramic view, go to your right where you see the collection of twelve massive white columns.

___ 6. When you reach the twelve columns, you will face two massive buildings, which you will walk toward and then in between.

___ 7. From the large columns in the courtyard of the buildings mentioned in note 6, go left.

___ 8. When you reach the Tour (tower) Belvédère you will see Cergy-St-Christophe's store-lined main street. Walk down this street to the train station, which is directly beneath the huge clock.

Suggestions for More Walking

To shorten this walk by about two miles, skip the walk along the Oise River and walk southwest directly along the waymarked path to Port-de-Cergy. You will see the waymarks on the shopping center level as you ascend from the RER station on the escalator. (From the place Charles de Gaulle you will begin on the Sere-Depoin.) For a two-mile extension, take the train to Pontoise from the Gare du Nord or Gare St-Lazare in Paris. Walk down to the Oise River, turn right and walk into Cergy-Préfecture, returning to the Oise via the path described above. For a very long day (about 13 miles), it is possible to combine this walk with the walk from Pontoise to Auvers-sur-Oise.

Walk 29: Saint-Germain-en-Laye

Walk: Saint-Germain-en-Laye to Maisons-Laffitte

General Description

120 mins. 5.7 miles (9.2 km)

Saint-Germain-en-Laye will be on your short list of must-see sites around Paris. This is a pleasant town, not far from Paris via the RER, where a uniformed, multi-lingual police officer stands near the RER station ready to aid baffled tourists in locating local landmarks. The *château* is the main attraction and is worthy of delaying your walk for a couple of hours. Originally constructed doing the twelfth century, the *château* was entirely rebuilt during the sixteenth century and now houses the Musée des Antiquités Nationales. Some of the most famous pieces from prehistoric France are housed here; if you have walked in the Dordogne and visited some of the prehistoric sites, you will now be able to inspect many of the Dordogne's treasures from the remote past. After visiting the *château*, you will walk along the Grande Terrasse (2.4 kilometers), which was built under the direction of the master garden designer Le Notre in the seventeenth century and offers outstanding views of Paris. At the end of the Grande Terrasse you will plunge into the emerald-green solitude of the Forêt Domaniale de Saint-Germain-en-Laye. As you emerge from the forest, you will enter Maisons-Laffitte, which is home to another venerable *château* constructed early in the reign of Louis XIV. Visit the *château*, have lunch, and return rapidly to Paris via the RER.

Optional Maps/topo-guides: Série Bleue 2214 (TOP 25) ET Versailles Forêts de Marly et de St-Germain; GR 1 (reference #101) Sentier de l'Ile-de-France (pp. 149–152) (*Footpaths of France Series: Walks 'Round Paris*)

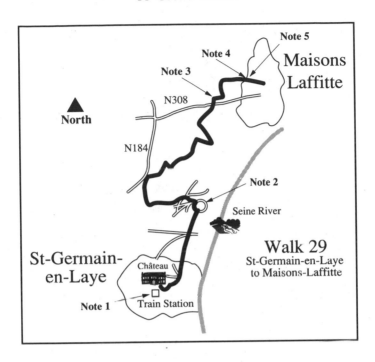

Time/Distance: 2 hours/5.7 miles (9.2 kilometers)

Difficulties: None

Toilet Facilities: None, but some privacy

Refreshments: Restaurants and cafés at Saint-Germain-en-Laye and Maisons-Laffitte

Getting There: From Paris, take the RER line A to Saint-Germain-en-Laye.

Trail Notes

____ 1a. When you exit from the train, walk behind the *château*, which is next to the station.

____ 1b. Turn left at avenue Le Notre and enter the grounds of the *château* through a small gate.

___ 1c. Turn right and walk until you reach the end of the grounds and have a great view of Paris and La Défense.

___ 1d. Turn left on the broad road that over looks the Seine for 2.4 kilometers called "La Terrasse." There are no waymarks on this section of the walk.

___ 2a. When you reach the end of La Terrasse (you will arrive at a circle of trees), turn left and go through a small doorway which is next to a large gate.

___ 2b. The door that you pass through is next to a building called "Maison Forestière de la Grille Royale." You will see a change-direction waymark at this point. Go straight on the asphalt road.

___ 2c. You will then see a diverticulum waymark (regular waymark with a vertical line through it) where you will turn right.

___ 3a. As soon as you pass N308 (about 1 hour 25 minutes), which is a major road, start looking right.

___ 3b. About 2 to 3 minutes beyond N308, you will see a change-direction waymark that indicates a left turn. Important: Do not go left; look right and you will see a diverticulum waymark. Go right, and begin looking left. You will soon see a waymark indicating a left turn.

___ 3c. About seven minutes later you will turn right. The turn is marked but easy to miss.

___ 4. Just outside of Maisons Laffitte, watch for a fork where you will turn right.

___ 5. Emerging from the forest, you will pass houses and apartments. When you come to a dead end, take a quick left and then a quick right. Continue down this street (rue St-Nicholas) which will take you to the train station.

Suggestions for More Walking

Although it is impossible to shorten this walk via public transportation, you may continue the same trail through Maisons Laffitte and on into Archères-Ville which marks the end of this portion of GR 1 and adds another 5.6 miles to the walk.

Walk 30: Fontainebleau: The Fabulous Forest

Walk: Fontainebleau to Bois-le-Rois

115 mins.
6.2 miles (10 km)

General Description

After Versailles, Fontainebleau is prob-
ably the most celebrated *château* in France. This site long served
as a hunting lodge for French kings who slowly added a variety
of buildings. Almost all traces of previous buildings had disappeared when, during the sixteenth century, François I had the
present palace built. The splendid exterior is matched by the carefully restored rooms that are open to the public. Visit the sometimes crowded *château* and then walk into the renowned and
beautiful Forêt de Fontainebleau, where you will leave the crowds
behind. This enchanting forest walk will lead you to the town of
Bois-le-Rois, which lurks sleepily on the edge of the forest. There
is nothing to do here except enjoy the views of the Seine and
relax in one of the few cafés.

Optional Maps/topo-guides: Série Bleue 2417 (TOP 25) Forêt de
Fontainebleau; no topo-guide

Time/Distance: 1 hour 55 minutes/6.2 miles (10 kilometers)

Difficulties: None

Toilet Facilities: None, but much privacy

Refreshments: Restaurants and cafés at Fontainebleau and Bois-le-
Rois

Getting There: The trains for Fontainebleau depart from the Gare
de Lyon in Paris. Currently, a train for Fontainebleau leaves from
quai 11 every hour to 1 hour 15 minutes

Trail Notes

___ 1a. When you leave the train, take the underground passage to the other side of the tracks where the station is located.

___ 1b. Emerging from the station, you will see the bus stop where you can board a bus to the *château*. From the bus stop (you are still in the train station parking lot), go directly right: you will see some stairs leading up that are marked with a red and white diverticulum waymark (regular waymark with a vertical line drawn through it).

___ 1c. When you arrive at the top of the stairs, cross the street and go left. You will see a diverticulum waymark and also a green and white waymark. You will be walking along the train tracks and after about 4 to 5 minutes, the red and white waymark indicates a left turn. Important: Do not go left. You will continue straight and follow the green and white waymarks.

___ 2. About 15 minutes into the walk, you will turn left. There is no change-direction waymark here so continue to look left for a path that has trees on both sides; it is marked with the green and white waymarks.

___ 3. When you pass D116 (about 50 minutes into the walk), which is an asphalt road indicated by a yellow line on the Série Bleu map, begin to look right at every trail. You will see a waymark, but it is very faded. The trail is called "route de Faon."

___ 4. About 90 minutes into the walk, you will come to a clearing which is called "Carrefour des Ventes du Bouchard." This is where you will leave the marked trail. The marked trail goes to the left but you will continue straight on the trail that you are on. About 4 to 5 minutes later, you will turn right onto an asphalt road called "Route du Pavé de la Cave," which takes you into Bois-le-Rois.

___ 5. Just before the concrete bridge over the road, turn left and you will arrive at the train station almost immediately.

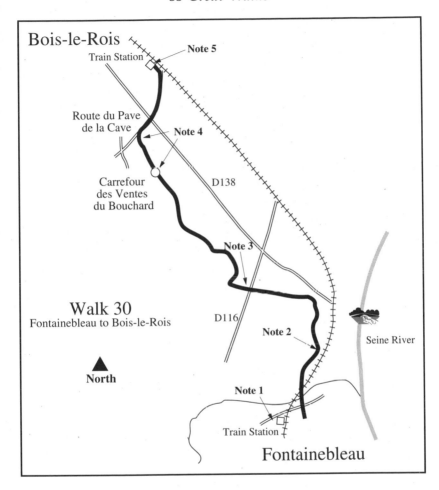

Bois-le-Rois

Train Station

Note 5

Route du Pave
de la Cave

Note 4

Carrefour
des Ventes
du Bouchard

D138

Note 3

Walk 30
Fontainebleau to Bois-le-Rois

D116

Note 2

Seine River

▲
North

Note 1

Train Station

Fontainebleau

Suggestions for More Walking

Although it is not possible to shorten this walk via public transportation, you may combine this walk with the following walk to Melun for a total of 11.2 miles. Another pleasant walk through the Forêt de Fontainebleau involves exiting the same train just beyond Fontainebleau at Moret-sur-Loing and following the GR 11 into Fontainebleau (about nine miles).

Walk 31: A Walk Along the Seine

Walk: Bois-le-Rois to Melun

General Description

100 mins. **5 miles (8 km)**

Today's walk will seldom stray from the shores of the Seine River. The sight of Bois-le-Rois' elegant riverside homes, in an assortment of architectural styles, is itself worthy of the walk. However, the Seine, with its tree-lined banks, flotilla of slow moving barges, and serene swans, will constantly compete for your attention.

Melun, formerly a Roman city, now radiates from both banks of the Seine. There are no sites of great note here but Melun is an agreeable lunch-stop town. If you have time, visit the museum, which at one time served as a home to Louis XIV's finance minister, the convicted embezzler Fouquet, who was later imprisoned at the Château de Vincennes and guarded by d'Artagnan of Three Musketeers fame.

Optional Maps/topo-guides: Série Bleue 2417 OT (TOP 25) Forêt de Fontainebleau/ 2415 OT (TOP 25) Evry/Melun; GR 1 (reference #101) Sentier de l'Ile-de-France

Time/Distance: 1 hour 40 minutes/5 miles (8 kilometers)

Difficulties: None

Toilet Facilities: None, but some privacy

Refreshments: Restaurants and cafés at Bois-le-Rois and Melun

Getting There: The trains for Bois-le-Rois depart from the Gare de Lyon (same line as Fontainebleau). Currently, a train leaves from quai 11 every hour to 1 hour 15 minutes.

Trail Notes

___ 1a. When you exist at Bois-le-Rois, you will be on the opposite side of the tracks from the train station. Go to the bottom of the stairs where you will see a sign indicating "GR 1" and "GR 2"; follow the arrow for GR 2.

___ 1b. From the stairs, turn right and then turn left at the first street (avenue Paul Doumer), which is marked, and follow the waymarks.

___ 1c. About 8 to 9 minutes from the train station turn left down the road just before the bridge. You will then follow the Seine for about an hour.

___ 2. When you come to a sign that indicates "La Rochette," both the waymarks and the Série Bleu map indicate that you should go left and up along the railroad tracks. However, I continued straight ahead down the road that skirts the Seine and was rewarded by views of the Seine and splendid mansions. I also received a bonus wind from the river. As you will note on the map, this road will soon join the official trail.

___ 3. About 1 hour 25 minutes into the walk, as you approach Melun, you will turn left on avenue de la Libération. This turn is not clearly marked so watch carefully. This street takes you directly to the train station.

Suggestions for More Walking

Although it is not possible to shorten this walk via public transportation, you may combine this walk with walk 30 for a total of 11.2 miles. About five miles northeast of Melun, along the GR 1, lies the magnificent Château de Vaux-le-Vicomte, which belonged to finance minister Fouquet and stunned the youthful Louis XIV, who jealously had Fouquet thrown in jail assuming embezzlement on a grand scale. Buses run to Maincy, where you can take a 3.5-mile round-trip walk to the *château* or walk from Melun to the *château* and then back to Maincy, where you can catch the bus

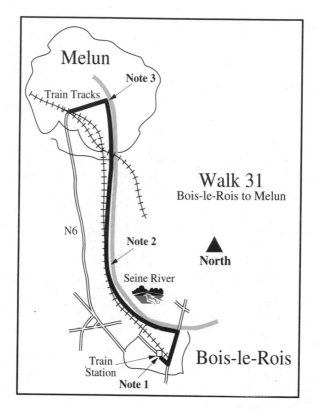

back to Melun for a total of 6.5 miles. Alternatively, you can take a taxi to the *château* and walk back the five miles to Melun.

Walk 32: Versailles: The Great Palace

Walk: **Versailles to Saint-Cyr-l'Ecole**

General Description

120 mins.
6 miles (9.6 km)

Beyond the Paris city limits, the ostentatious palace of Versailles is probably France's most-visited historical site. Built by the dictator Louis XIV with little regard for the crushing burden imposed on his subjects, Versailles stands as a symbol of absolute power corrupting absolutely. Perhaps, however, Louis was just being far-sighted and realized that one day France would need the tourist dollars that historic monuments draw. I doubt Louis' prescience; but if you are in Paris, you will visit his palace. After standing in line, sometimes for hours, and colliding with DROPS being herded from one gilded and ornate chamber to the next, you will be ardent in your desire to walk away from the crowds. Ten minutes from the palace, as you enter the Forêt Domaniale de Versailles, you will have left the other tourists far behind. As they board tourist buses, or scurry to secure a prized seat on public transportation, or search in vain for their towed-away automobiles, you will be walking calmly through forests and along lakes. Bring something for lunch, and lounge at one of the many lake-side picnic tables. Departing from the forest, feeling much better for having walked, you will enter St-Cyr-l'Ecole, where there is nothing to do but lounge at a café and return to Paris on the RER.

Optional Maps/topo-guides: Série Bleue 2214 ET (TOP 25); PR/G (reference #043) A la Découverte des Yvelines (pp. 122–123)

Time/Distance: 2 hours/6 miles (10 kilometers)

Difficulties: Some minor climbs

Toilet Facilities: None, but some privacy

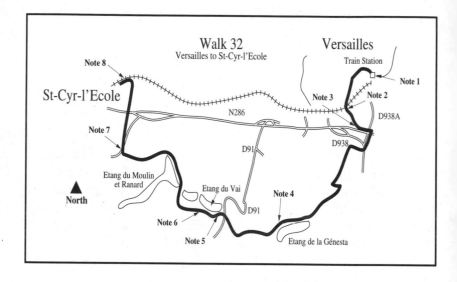

Refreshments: Restaurants and cafés at Versailles and Saint-Cyr-l'Ecole

Getting There: Take the RER line C-7 to Versailles-Chantiers

Trail Notes

___ 1a. From the station, walk straight ahead. You will see a red and white diverticulum waymark on a lamp post which you will follow straight until you reach N186 (rue des Etats Généraux), where you turn left.

___ 1b. You will turn left again at the first street (rue de Noailles), which later becomes rue Edouard Charton. (If you visit the *château* before completing the walk to Saint-Cyr-l'Ecole, walk from the *château* on avenue Sceaux and turn right where it ends at rue Edouard Charton.)

___ 2. After you cross a bridge over the railroad tracks, turn left (you will see a waymark) and then take a quick right.

__ 3a. Just before you reach N286, a very busy road, turn left on a narrow trail; you will soon turn right again and go beneath N286.

__ 3b. A couple of minutes after you cross under N286, you will cross another narrow road, D938. Here you can go left or right at a fork. Take the path to your right. Important: A couple of minutes after this fork, you will come to a tree which has a yellow waymark indicating straight ahead and a red and white waymark that indicates left. Follow the red and white waymark, and go left.

__ 4. About an hour into the walk, after you have passed the first small lake (Etang de la Géneste), you will be walking on a wide dirt trail. Follow this trail as it turns left and then turn right when you come to an asphalt road a couple of minutes later. About 100 yards down the asphalt road, you will see a waymark.

__ 5. When you arrive at the second small lake (Etang du Val), descend to the trail that follows the lake.

__ 6. When you leave the trail that goes around Etang du Val, go left and up into the forest where you will see waymarks.

__ 7. About 1 hour 45 minutes into the walk, after you have just crossed a bridge over an expressway, you will see a change-direction waymark indicating a left turn. Important: Do not go in this direction. Turn right where you see the diverticulum waymark (regular waymark with vertical line through it) which will take you directly to the train station at Saint-Cyr-l'Ecole. (Caution: Do not follow the yellow waymarks which go to the right, unless you wish to walk back to Versailles. Continue to follow the red and white diverticulum waymarks.)

__ 8. When you turn left before the train station at Saint-Cyr-l'Ecole, begin to look right for an underground passage that leads you directly to the station.

Suggestions for More Walking

Although there is no possibility of shortening this walk via public transportation, you may continue along GR 11 beyond Saint-Cyr-l'Ecole to either Les Clayes-sous-Bois or Plaisir (same map/topo-guide) where you will find train stations, adding either six miles or ten miles to the walk. You may also approach Versailles from the north (same map) from Vaucresson (about three miles), Louveciennes (about five miles), Marly-le-Roi (about 7.5 miles), or even Saint-Germain-en-Laye (about 20 miles).

Walk 33: A Walk Along the Marne

Walk: Lagny-sur-Marne to Esbly

130 mins.
6.2 miles (10 km)

General Description

Lagny-sur-Marne lies recumbent and remote along its slow-moving river. Visit the well-preserved, thirteenth-century church; wander about the agreeable town for a few minutes; cross the bridge over the Marne River; and enter the silence of the non-vehicular world. Paris will be far from your thoughts as you walk through the verdant countryside with the Marne almost always in view. Many antiquated barges converted to recreational use (another group of anomalous conveyances worthy of some future when-all-land-has-sunken-into-the-sea Mad Max film) will plod past you at a pace barely faster than you can walk. It may seem that they are having more fun; but, remember, you are getting exercise while they are growing flabby. You will add to the supernatural flotilla of barges another other-worldly experience: an outdoor museum featuring faceless, animal-like monumental statuary that appears to have Mayan or perhaps Martian origins. I suspect that future archaeologists will consider these to be solid evidence that the earth was once settled by visitors from outer space or that France was at one time conquered by Mayan

invaders. You will also pass by the birthplace of Louis Braille just off the trail in Coupvray, where the inventor of the reading system for the blind's home has been converted into a small museum. Esbly, along the Marne, is a pleasant terminus for this walk and a suitable place to re-enter twentieth-century Earth.

Optional Maps/topo-guides: Série Bleue 2414 ET (TOP 25); Marne-la-Vallée; GR 14A (reference #113) Sentier de la Marne (I have seen this little guide only at the FFRP bookstore, 64 Rue de Gergovie, Paris 75014)

Time/Distance: 2 hours 10 minutes/6.2 miles (10 kilometers)

Difficulties: One short climb; parts of the canal trail are overgrown and dense foliage can scratch those who wear shorts.

Toilet Facilities: None, but much privacy

Refreshments: Restaurants and cafés at Lagny-sur-Marne and Esbly. There is also another restaurant which caters to boaters about midway, near a set of locks.

Getting There: Trains for Lagny leave from the Gare de l'Est in Paris about every thirty minutes. Look on the map between platforms 16 and 17 to see which train goes to Lagny. If you are in doubt, ask.

Trail Notes

___ 1. From the train station at Lagny, go directly ahead on rue du Maréchal Foch. You will see a bridge which you will use to cross the Marne River. Turn left as soon as you cross the bridge onto quai Saint Père.

___ 2. About 15 minutes into the walk, you will encounter a waymark that indicates that you should turn away from the *quai* at a place called "Square Ste-Agathe-des-Montes." I ignored those waymarks so that I could stay on the riverside path. I suggest that you do the same since the walk along the river is more interesting, and you will soon rejoin the trail.

___ 3. When you arrive at Chessy, continue to follow the asphalt road called "Chemin de Meaux" until you arrive at the above mentioned outdoor museum where you turn left and walk back to the river bank. Where you reach the river, turn right and continue along the riverside trail.

___ 4. About 1 hour 15 minutes into the walk you will pass a canal lock. Follow the waymarks which will take you up and behind the large restaurant which you will soon see.

___ 5. About 1 hour 20 minutes into the walk, you will be descending from the only hill on this trail. You will see a change-direction waymark. Be certain to cross the asphalt road and descend on the dirt trail just beyond. This trail winds its way to the canal path which you will soon continue on.

___ 6. About 1 hour 35 minutes into the trail, you will see a way-

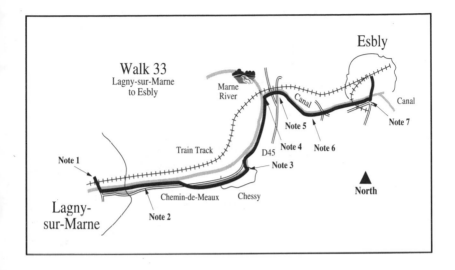

mark that takes you away from the river. Feel free to ignore its since it takes you back to the bank almost immediately. You will encounter the same situation a few minutes later; again, you can ignore the waymark.

___ 7. Turn left onto a large green metal bridge about 2 hours into the walk. You have reached Esbly and will see a diverticulum waymark that will lead you to the train station, which you will reach a few minutes later.

Suggestions for More Walking

Although it is not possible to shorten this walk via public transportation, it is possible to continue an extra 2.5 miles from Esbly along an attractive canal to Couilly-Pont-aux-Dames, where there is a train station, or down to Crécy-la-Chapelle (total of about 14.5 miles from Lagny) where there it also a station.

Walk 34: In the Footsteps of the Impressionists

Walk: Pontoise to Auvers-sur-Oise

General Description

**125 mins.
6 miles (9.6 km)**

The walk to Auvers-sur-Oise will be a pilgrimage for students of art history. This picturesque town, which describes itself as being the "cradle of Impressionism" in its tourist literature, has hosted the artists Daubigny, Cézanne, Pissarro, Rousseau, Vlaminck, and many others. Vincent Van Gogh spent the last months of his life here where he zealously completed more than seventy canvases. He committed suicide near the town hall in a small mansard where he was living and he is buried in the cemetery near the church that he made famous in his painting *L'église d'Auvers*. The tourist office has a brochure that will guide you through the town where numerous plaques, featuring reproductions and descriptions of artists' works, are erected at the now famous sites.

Pontoise was also a favorite of Impressionist artists; Pissarro painted here for almost two decades. The town is home to a fifteenth-century cathedral and also the Musée Pissarro which is at the lofty site of the now-vanished *château*. The views of the Oise River and Pontoise from the *château* ground's high promontory are an excellent prelude for today's walk, which will take you from the heights of Pontoise, along the Oise River, and through the hamlets, farms, and wheat fields that have been immortalized by many great artists.

Optional Maps/topo-guides: Série Bleu (TOP 25) 2313 OT Forêts de Montmorency de L'Isle-Adam et de Carnelle; GR 1 (reference #101) Sentier de l'Ile-de-France (pp. 40–45) (*Footpaths of France Series: Walks 'Round Paris*)

Time/Distance: 2 hours 5 minutes/6 miles (9.6 kilometers)

Difficulties: Several short climbs

Toilet Facilities: None, but much privacy

Refreshments: Restaurants and cafés at Pontoise and Auvers-sur-Oise

Getting There: Trains for Pontoise depart Paris' Gare Saint-Lazare from platforms 8–12.

Trail Notes

NOTE: This is a good trail to purchase the Série Bleu map, since it is occasionally difficult to follow, particularly through the open fields. However, the trail notes should get you to Auvers-sur-Oise without too much difficulty.

___ 1. The easiest way to begin this walk is to simply turn right onto the first street (rue Sere Depoin) past the place Général

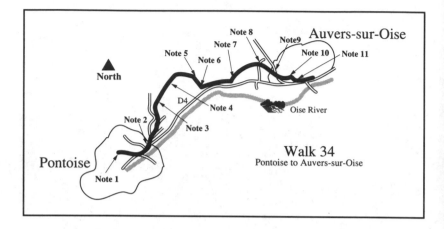

de Gaulle that runs parallel with the train station and the railroad tracks, following this road down to the Oise River where you will turn left on the quai du Pothuis. Alternatively, visit the town and make your way down to the Oise River where you turn left (do not cross the bridge to the other side of the Oise River), and walk along the river on the quai du Pothuis.

___ 2a. About 10 minutes from the train station, turn left on D927 (rue de l'Hermitage).

___ 2b. Then at the first traffic light, turn right onto rue Adrien-LeMoine.

___ 2c. At the top of this street, you will see a fork; bear left onto the Chemin Bois-Payen.

___ 2d. When you pass the last house, turn left onto a trail and into the woods.

___ 3. About 40 minutes into the walk, you will come out of a wooded area where you will see some office buildings. You will then come to an asphalt road and will see a bus stop. Cross the road going slightly left, continuing straight ahead back into the forest. You will see a red and orange waymark on a concrete utility pole that brings you back into the woods. Continue straight ahead; you will soon see the first of the red and white waymarks that will bring you into Auvers-sur-Oise. (Note: You will soon see a fork where you will bear to the right—going left along a fence will take you in the wrong direction; it is well marked)

___ 4. Important: After having crossed the area described in note 3, you will leave the woods for a second time. You will see a waymark that indicates that you go straight, then right, and then left in 200 meters. Therefore, as you traverse the trail through open fields, you will go right at the first intersecting trail and then left at the next intersecting trail which occurs almost immediately (there is no place to leave a waymark at either turn). You will soon see a waymark on a fence.

___ 5a. When you come to the third trail intersection (after having crossed the intersection described in note 4), you must go right; you will see a waymark on a tree almost immediately.

___ 5b. After you have made this right turn, continue to look left. About three minutes later, you will turn left and down into the forest (you will see a waymark).

___ 6. About 1 hour 5 minutes into the walk, you will take a well-marked left turn which takes you past a house. When you reach the end of the house, you have the choice of going left and up or right and level. Go left and up; you will soon see a waymark.

___ 7a. About 1 hours 30 minutes into the walk, you will have the choice of going left along a road called chemin des Monts or right along chemin des Muliers. I took the official route along chemin des Monts, but a local resident told me that the other road also leads to Auvers-sur-Oise and the map confirms this (a slightly shorter variation if you are tired or in a hurry).

___ 7b. As you walk along chemin des Monts, watch to your left for a place where you will turn left, and make a short climb over some rocky terrain (the turn is clearly marked). When you get to the top, turn right along a grassy path; there is no waymark until you reach a patch of woods.

___ 8. About 1 hour 40 minutes into the walk, you will come to an asphalt road. Just cross and continue straight on your present path; you will soon see a waymark.

___ 9. When you reach D928 (about 1 hour 45 minutes), a paved road, go right and down. Soon you will turn left (you will see a waymark) and walk along the grounds of a *château*.

___ 10. When you reach the rue Daubigny, turn right into town. You will see a diverticulum waymark. (Do not go left where you see the regular waymarks.)

___ 11. Soon after you pass the tourist office (*syndicat d'initiative*), you will come to a traffic light at the main road. Turn left; the train station is about 5 minutes down the road. Take the train or bus back to Pontoise where a train leaves for Paris.

Suggestions for More Walking

A good way to lengthen this walk by about 2.5 miles is to take RER line A3 to Cergy-Préfecture, walk down to the Oise on the boulevard de l'Oise, turn left and follow the Oise River into Pontoise. There is no possibility of shortening this walk by using public transportation; however, it is possible to approach Auvers-sur-Oise from L'Isle-Adam (accessible from Paris' Gare du Nord) in only about 4.5 miles of frequent riverside walking, or also about 10 miles via Nesles-la-Vallée. Use the same Série Bleu map mentioned above.

Walk 35: The End of the RER

Walk: Sermaise to Dourdan

General Description

105 mins. 5 miles (8 km)

Sermaise is a quiet little village hidden from urban perils near the Orge River about thirty miles from Paris. Walking through this flowery, perfectly-groomed town with its narrow lanes and ivy-covered homes, you would never suspect that you are within commuting distance of Paris on the RER (if you have ever spent sleepless nights wondering about what lies at the end of the RER, this walk will restore you to restful slumber). This part of the Ile-de-France, not yet disfigured by crowds of tourists, has maintained its traditional lifestyles and appearances.

The route to Dourdan is a delightful trek through leafy forests, gentle hills, fertile fields, and serene hamlets. Dourdan, with its heavily fortified, well-preserved thirteenth-century *château*, extensive town walls, and impressively large twelfth-century church, serves as this superb walk's worthy culmination.

Optional Maps/topo-guides: Série Bleu 2216 ET (TOP 25) Etampes Dourdan; GR 1 (reference #101) Sentier de l'Ile-de-France (pp. 121–124) (*Footpaths of France Series: Walks 'Round Paris*)

Time/Distance: 1 hour 45 minutes/5 miles (8 kilometers)

Difficulties: One climb out of Sermaise

Toilet Facilities: None, but some privacy

Refreshments: Restaurants and cafés at Sermaise and Dourdan

Getting There: From Paris, take the RER line C4 to Sermaise.

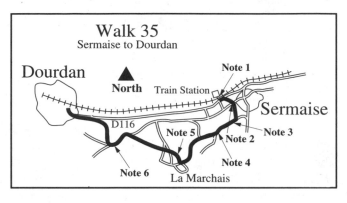

Walk 35
Sermaise to Dourdan

Dourdan ▲ North Train Station

Note 1

Sermaise

D116 Note 5 Note 2 Note 3

Note 4

Note 6 La Marchais

Trail Notes

___ 1a. From the RER stop at Sermaise, cross D116, turn left and then right onto the first intersecting asphalt road called chemin de Pont de Bois.

___ 1b. When you reach the next intersecting road, turn left into Sermaise which you will see just ahead.

___ 2. About 10 minutes from the RER stop, you will reach the church of Sermaise; turn right on rue de la Grosse Haie and you will see a waymark ahead on a pole.

___ 3. As you leave Sermaise, you will be walking uphill. As you approach the top, you will have a fence to your right and a field to your left. When you get near the top of the hill, turn right and continue to follow the fence. You will soon be on a narrow asphalt road. The waymarks on this portion of the trail have been painted over, but you are going in the correct direction.

___ 4. Just after a large farm complex (the first you will see), you will turn right off the asphalt road onto a dirt trail. The dirt trail will take you to the flowery village La Bruyère. When you reach a dead end, turn right and then take a quick left on the chemin des Gouttières, which takes you to the next village, La Marchais (just stay on the wide dirt track that skirts the forest and do not enter the forest to get to La Marchais).

___ 5. After passing La Marchais, you will be descending down a dirt road and will see a waymark and two wooden signs indicating "Poissard" and "Beaurepaire." You will then quickly come to a fork where you will see no waymark. Go left onto a grassy trail where you will soon see a waymark on a tree.

___ 6a. About 1 hour 15 minutes into the walk you will be walking along an asphalt road (chemin de Beaurepaire) and will emerge at a major intersection with a traffic circle. You will see a waymark that indicates a right turn. Walk right along the traffic circle and turn right at the first road. There is presently, due to recent construction, no waymark here. Walk down the side of the street that has a sidewalk. To your left, you will see a park and a camp ground surrounded by a fence.

___ 6b. When you come to the end of the camp ground, turn left.

___ 6c. When you come to a fork, go right onto rue Gaston Lesage. After this point the trail is well marked and follows successively avenue de Paris, rue Gautreau, boulevard des Allies, avenue Carnot, and avenue du Dr Jules Bals up to the train station at Dourdan.

Suggestions for More Walking

Although this walk is impossible to shorten via public transportation, it is possible to exit at the station just before Sermaise, St-Cheron and walk along the same trail dotted with picturesque villages (also the same map/topo-guide) to Dourdan adding about five miles to the days walk.

Suggestions for Other Walks Around Paris

If you are seeking some longer walks, try the walk from Pont de Saint-Cloud (just outside Paris and the starting point for GR 1) to

Marly-le-Rois (17 kilometers/11 miles; GR 1 Sentier de l'Ile-de-France, pp. 19–24), which cuts through territory frequently painted by the Impressionists. You could also take the woodsy walk from Marly-le-Roi to Saint-Germain-en-Laye (20 kilometers/12.4 miles; same guide, pp. 24–27 and pp. 145–149). If you visit the Château de Chantilly, not too far by train from Paris, walk the 12 kilometers (7.5 miles) to the well-preserved medieval town of Senlis, have lunch, look around town, and take the bus back to Chantilly (GR 11–11C reference #121 Ile-de-France Fontainebleau-Senlis, pp. 65–67 or IGN TOP 25 map 2412 OT Forêts de Chantilly d'Hallatte et d'Ermenonville). Paris's great parks, Bois de Vincennes and Bois de Boulogne, also offer some outstanding walks, and the Château de Vincennes with its wax figures portraying prisoners, guards, and others is itself worth the metro ride to the park. If you wish to follow waymarked trails ranging from 2 to 11 kilometers, purchase the guide *GR de Pays: A la Découverte des Bois de Paris*; otherwise, any map of the park will be suitable. Backpackers can walk forever on the trails around Paris. Accommodations are frequent, and you are usually within reach of some form of public transportation linked to Paris.